ARCHITECTURAL DIGEST
HOLLYWOOD AT HOME

ARCHITECTURAL DIGEST
HOLLYWOOD AT HOME

HARRY N. ABRAMS, INC., PUBLISHERS

Editor: Andrea Danese
Designer: Miko McGinty
Production Manager: Maria Pia Gramaglia

Library of Congress Control Number: 2005928190

Printed and bound in China
10 9 8 7 6 5 4 3 2 1

Harry N. Abrams, Inc.
100 Fifth Avenue
New York, N.Y. 10011
www.abramsbooks.com

Abrams is a subsidiary of

LA MARTINIÈRE
GROUPE

Contents

Preface

A Hollywood State of Mind

BY PAIGE RENSE

This book really began in 1970, the year I became editor of *Architectural Digest*, when it was a little-known West Coast magazine. It was not remotely as it is today, but that is another story. In 1970 it seemed essential that *Architectural Digest* become well known nationally and, not incidentally, internationally, to survive in the competitive world of magazine publishing. We wanted people to talk about the magazine, and one way to create talk was to show the homes of Hollywood's celebrities. People did talk. They are still talking.

This book is composed primarily of editorial material that appeared in the pages of *Architectural Digest* throughout the last several decades. Now Hollywood is no longer Hollywood. Movies are made all over the world, and stars live everywhere. Hollywood has always existed far beyond geographic boundaries. Hollywood is a state of mind. A dream state. However, the people who star in those dreams actually live in reality—their own reality, reflected in their homes. Several are fantastical. Cher's Malibu home is one example, and you will see our version of Haydn's *Surprise Symphony* on pages 116–125.

Perhaps the most telling difference in the way Hollywood lived then and now is exemplified by the residences of three blonde stars: Jean Harlow, platinum and satin, pure movie star fantasy; Marilyn Monroe, who first dreamed of stardom, then intellectual acceptance, and died only a few months after finding her first real home; then there's Candice Bergen, whose intelligence and inter-

ests have always been reflected in her houses. She, Diane Keaton, and Anjelica Huston are three of today's female stars who are clear about who they are and the way they want to live. Cary Grant and Randolph Scott were clear about the way they wanted to live (roommates or more?), gossip be damned. John Wayne lived with his boat in his backyard, which happened to be the Pacific Ocean. (The boat was away for repairs when he showed us through his house. Also away, he said, was a dinosaur's foot.)

Every living person in this book was gracious and cooperative, both stars and directors, especially two who went the extra mile for a great shoot: Dennis Quaid, who produced fireworks, and John Travolta, who produced jets. A belated thank you to Dena Kaye, whose father, Danny, once cooked a Chinese dinner for us. And on behalf of the talented *AD* staff, thanks to all the wonderful writers and photographers whose contributions to *Architectural Digest* made this book possible. A special thank you to James Munn, whose knowledge of movie history and dedicated research helped make *Hollywood at Home* a reality. And one more thank you to all those at Harry N. Abrams who shared our enthusiasm.

Presenting Anjelica Huston and her father, John, in this book forged a historical link between Hollywood and its magical people, stars, and directors, past and present. The tenuous magic that draws us into the aura of the personality is what this book is all about— *Hollywood at Home*.

Introduction

BY GERALD CLARKE

A machine, it is said, has no emotions. But every cine-matographer knows better. The movie camera loves some people, it hates others, and Hollywood studios have made and lost fortunes trying to determine which ones it will favor—and which it won't. Beauty helps, of course, but it is never enough. That quixotic instrument has admired a slightly pop-eyed Bette Davis as much as a flawless Lana Turner, a homely Humphrey Bogart as much as a handsome Cary Grant. Only one thing can be said for certain: the camera is an infallible judge. The performer who captures its heart will, with almost math-ematical certainty, also capture the hearts of millions of others and go on to become one of the rarest creatures on earth—a movie star.

The camera's—and the public's—fascination with movie stars extends even into the way they live. A house that might escape notice if it belonged to a banker, a doc-tor, or a lawyer becomes an object of intense interest if it is a star's address. Who would pass up an opportunity to stroll through Frank Sinatra's Palm Springs compound? Peek into Marilyn Monroe's bedroom? Or watch the flames dance in the massive living room fireplace of Ronald and Nancy Reagan? This book is thus not just a volume of words and pictures. It is an invitation into the movie world's inner sanctums. In the pages that follow you will sit in the living room of Jean Harlow, browse through the many titles in Jimmy Stewart's library, and gaze at the moon and planets from Dennis Quaid's miniature observatory in Montana.

Most of the homes you will visit are, of course, in Southern California, where the motion picture industry grew up and where it has been centered for nearly a century. Several are in New York City, where movies are also made and where many stars prefer to live. Others are scattered in choice spots around the United States, from Katharine Hepburn's rambling country house—"my paradise," she called it—on Long Island Sound in Connecticut to John Travolta's sprawling one-story in Florida, which has two jets, a Boeing 707, and a Gulfstream II, parked near the door, just in case the airplane-happy actor feels the urge to have dinner in Paris or New York. A few belong not to stars, but to star makers: Golden Age directors such as Cecil B. DeMille and George Cukor, together with two of their most renowned descendants, Martin Scorsese and Steven Spielberg.

The design styles you will see on your tour through these pages vary as much as the acting styles you will see on the screen. Diane Keaton's Spanish Colonial in Bel-Air mirrors the unpretentious, down-to-earth person-ality of the lead in *Annie Hall*. Anjelica Huston's house in Venice—the California Venice, that is—resembles a colorful modern sculpture, which is no surprise since it was designed by her sculptor husband, Robert Graham.

Just the opposite is Cecil B. DeMille's sumptuous Los Angeles mansion. With its vaulted ceilings, Persian carpets, and somber, dark woods, it reflects the conservative yet expansive tastes of one of the movie industry's founders. If DeMille, venturing west from New York, had shot *The Squaw Man* (1913) in Arizona, as he originally intended, rather than in California, as he eventually did, other filmmakers would probably have followed and Hollywood might now be known as Cactusville.

If design styles vary, the Hollywood elite's passion for excellence does not. Studio craftspeople have always been able to create sets that seem more real than reality. "I've been to Paris, France and I've been to Paris Paramount; Paris Paramount is better," joked Ernst Lubitsch, the director of such comic classics as *Ninotchka* and *To Be or Not to Be*. Accustomed to the best of the best in set and production designs, stars have demanded the same high-level of artistry in their homes. Typical is the young Judy Garland's New England-inspired house in Bel-Air. Set behind a white picket fence on a winding canyon road, it looks as if it belongs on a village green in Vermont. All that is missing to complete the illusion is snow, sleigh bells, and a simmering pot of clam chowder on the stove.

Not too long ago many Easterners looked down their noses at the strange ways of Hollywood. "Better Death in Venice than life in Hollywood," Truman Capote wrote during his first visit in 1947. It took a Parisian intellectual, Simone de Beauvoir, to peer through the snobbery and see that the Los Angeles of that era was, to use her words, "the most sophisticated city in the world," a place where Thomas Mann could rub shoulders with Greta Garbo, Bertolt Brecht with Cary Grant.

Many of those sophisticates came together in a home included here, George Cukor's art-filled house in the hills above Sunset Boulevard. It was there, in what the director called his Oval Room, that Katharine Hepburn once found herself on a crowded couch, sandwiched between Igor Stravinsky and Groucho Marx. Hepburn and Stravinsky wanted to talk about Australia's magnificent long-tailed lyrebirds, whose song the composer wanted to incorporate into a symphony. Marx wanted only to crack jokes, causing Hepburn to issue a series of sharp commands—"Shut up, Groucho! Shut up, Groucho!"

Listen carefully as you travel the years in the time machine you hold in your hand, and you can almost hear her brittle, high-pitched bark—along with Marilyn's sexy whisper, Clark Gable's gravelly baritone, and Judy Garland's nervous vibrato, ready any second to sing of an enchanted land over the rainbow and the man that got away. But shut up, Groucho: the tour is about to begin.

Candice Bergen

California Comforts for the Actress's Spanish-Style Residence in Los Angeles

TEXT BY SUSAN CHEEVER
PHOTOGRAPHY BY ROBERT RECK

Over the years she often explored the hidden cul-de-sac twisting down a hill between thick walls of ivy and creeping fig. One house fascinated her, although all she could see was a white chimney and a mysterious tile roof rising from masses of bougainvillea and avocado trees. "I had always been drawn to this house; it was vaguely Spanish, and I grew up in a Spanish house," says Candice Bergen. "Of course, when I finally looked at it as a buyer, I was shocked to see all this." She waves past the fountain and the stairs planted with orchids and agave, toward a grassy private valley where a gazebo peeks from a grove of fruit trees.

Candice Bergen has reinvented herself many times— as an actress in films directed by Sidney Lumet and Mike Nichols; as a writer whose memoir, *Knock Wood*, told about being the daughter of ventriloquist and comedian Edgar Bergen and the sister of puppet Charlie McCarthy; as television's unsinkable Murphy Brown; as the wife of the late film director Louis Malle; and as the mother of their daughter, Chloe. But she had never reinvented a house before. "I'd never done a real renovation," she says. "It was a massive and prolonged dose of stress: It was like a stress time-release capsule."

Bergen wanted a change from the nearby house where she had lived with her husband, who died of cancer in 1995. "After he died, I thought a lot about whether we should stay in Los Angeles," she says. "My mother and my brother are here, and it seemed very important to hold on to a sense of family. I was trying to compensate for what we've been through, to make an idyllic place for my daughter."

Transforming the original house into an idyllic place, however, seemed like a Spanish mission impossible. Below the white chimney was a narrow house built in 1941. "It was a maze of add-ons," says architect William Murray. "Each add-on went farther underground." The overgrown gardens were beyond a white picket fence and a small cliff. To open the house to the land, and to transform it into rooms where Bergen could live comfortably with her daughter, their two dogs, and a rotating cast of friends and guests, Murray took the house down to its

"I love Spanish houses— they're the only houses that make sense in Los Angeles," says Candice Bergen (ABOVE, with her dogs, Larry and Lois). The actress, who lives with her daughter, Chloe, renovated a hacienda-style residence in West Los Angeles that she'd admired as a child.

During the renovation, "I was thinking family, I was thinking new start," Bergen says. "Chloe is about to be a teenager, and I wanted her and her friends to hang out here." OPPOSITE: The low profile of the exterior disguises the interior volume. Column from Arté de Mexico.

walls, constructed a series of private terraces, and planned rooms joined by archways on four different levels. He carved a sitting room for the master bedroom out of a porch, built a tower with clerestory windows for the master bath, and created a new family room and kitchen around a huge Victorian box tree surrounded by white Stephanotis and glacier ivy. In the end, the renovations were so extensive and expensive that Bergen christened her new home "Casa Costa Mucho."

"She bought it because she wanted a change," says designer Linda Marder. "I said to myself, 'She's a widow, she's under an enormous amount of stress, and we'll make it perfect for her.'" While Murray drew plans for a light-filled central space, with a living room, dining room, and sitting room, Marder took Bergen shopping for reproduction Sultanabads and Ushaks in soft blue, red, and ivory patterns. They laid the rugs down on the rubble and began to choose colors, fabrics, and furniture, building the design from the ground up. "I call myself more a collaborator than a decorator," Marder says. "Candy has great taste." Nancy Kintisch came in to stencil and paint the walls and ceilings. Outside, Murray and landscape archi-

tect Richard Hayden created a secluded Shangri-la where paths curve past Santa Barbara daisies, jasmines, and lavender, and trellises by the swimming pool drip with bougainvillea. "When I first saw it, I had a glimpse of what it could be, a combination of Spanish and Moroccan," Bergen says. "I didn't realize that it was just a glimpse." "This design was about the intimacy of a small house," says Marder, who furnished it with reproductions, antiques, flea market finds, old fixtures, and pictures and objects from Bergen's life—prints of Egypt she and Malle collected, a camel-bone-and-coral chest bought in a Moroccan souk, an inlaid chair that was a gift from the *Murphy Brown* cast at the end of the series' decade-long run, inscribed "A Perfect Ten." An ornately carved Indian column is an introduction to the front door. A small entranceway, where a bench found for Bergen by the *Murphy Brown* set director sits under an iron chandelier, leads through an archway down steps to the living room.

Marder furnished the dining room with Queen Anne–style chairs and a peg-top cherry table from Los Angeles furniture maker Elijah Slocum. She hung an old California chandelier in front of a Maurice Braun land-

scape. "I love lamps," Bergen says. "Don't even talk to me about track lighting. I love lamps for the warmth they give a room, for the way the light comes through the shade." In the sitting room, which faces the gardens, Marder flanked a leather sofa with two red-lacquered Chinese chests. The space also includes an Anglo-Indian inlaid chair, a custom-made armchair and a nineteenth-century English table on which rests a bronze sculpture of a cheetah, made by T. D. Kelsey, that was given to Bergen by a friend.

"What's important to me in a house is that there's a tremendous sense of comfort," explains Bergen. "Every chair you sit in is comfortable. If you can't sit back, you're just in transit. If you're perched on a chair, you're perched to leave. Every table should be the type of table you can put your feet up on. Life is too short not to be comfortable." In the living room, Marder grouped sofas and chairs around a Giacometti-style iron-and-glass low table in front of the enormous fireplace. She separated the sofas with an English armchair and an inlaid Anglo-Indian table. On the ceiling beams Kintisch, working on a scaffold, stenciled a Mediterranean design. Over the mantelpiece, lit by candelabra and a Fortuny lamp, Marder hung a Dedrick Brandes Stuber painting. Sprays of white Phalaenopsis from Bergen's mother, Frances, droop toward the hand-forged fire screen.

ABOVE: Draperies section off the sleeping and sitting areas.

OPPOSITE: Architect William Murray installed book-shelves and paneling in the dining room.

Down several more steps, the master bedroom and its sitting room have their own terrace. On their walls Kintisch stenciled pale, abstract florals. A Regency cabinet and a leather bench at the end of the bed hold picture books on subjects from architecture to Zanzibar. "I like to have books around that you can actually open and read, as opposed to books piled up as a sculptural statement," Bergen says.

In the master bath, a sort of sitting room with silk-and-cotton-upholstered chairs, Marder decorated the tub with a large cement garden duck. "When I saw the duck, I knew Linda understood me," Bergen says. "I don't like houses that take themselves too seriously." Wherever Bergen lives, there are dogs on the furniture and a rubber chicken hanging from a chandelier—in this house it's in the breakfast room. "I can only be on my best behavior for so long," she says. "Then I need my rubber chicken. I need to laugh."

In this house she first saw so long ago, Bergen has found a new home for the woman she is right now. "As you get older, home becomes more important," she says. "You want to spend more time with friends. You're conscious of looking for a certain calm. Your priorities clarify themselves, and you're able to appreciate what you have."

OPPOSITE: "The rear terrace is one of the most important features of the house," Murray points out. "Each interior space opens onto it, and it acts as a living area and a circulation path to the rooms." A small fountain is adjacent to stairs leading to the lawn.

ABOVE: A view from the far garden takes in the house. "Candice wanted the garden to be natural, to have a little of that old California ranchy feeling," landscape architect Richard Hayden says.

Humphrey Bogart and Lauren Bacall

Stars of *To Have and Have Not* and *Key Largo*

BY MICHAEL FRANK

Cynical, arrogant, honest, brooding, notoriously tough and deeply but always secretly emotional (if a girl got lucky, he might tell her she's "good, awful good"), Humphrey Bogart's screen persona can be summed up as noble thug. Thug, of course, for all the marginal types he brought to life, the killers and the gangsters and even the cops who, in Bogart's rendition, were merely criminals who'd strayed to the other side of the law; noble for that brave and fiery independence—good guy or bad, Bogart was forever his own man.

The persona wasn't born with the person. The tight-jawed ruffian was actually the son of a physician and an illustrator. A student at the Trinity School in New York and the Phillips Academy in Andover, Massachusetts, from which he was expelled, and a seaman, second class, in the navy, where an injury to his mouth caused the famous lisp, Bogart began serving a long apprenticeship on the stage in 1920. He played a series of young men who "wore blazers, smiled a lot, and had impeccable manners," according to Lauren Bacall; reviewing his per-

BELOW: "We have six and a half acres here—I like the isolation," Humphrey Bogart said in 1952 of the ranch house he shared with wife Lauren Bacall in Benedict Canyon, California.

formance in *Swifty* (1922), Alexander Woollcott said (and later recanted) that Bogart's acting was "what is usually and mercifully described as inadequate." He made his film debut in a ten-minute short, *Broadway's Like That* (1930), and spent the next five years dividing his time between undistinguished B movies and additional roles on the stage, a talent in search of a niche.

This he found in 1935 in Duke Mantee, Robert Sherwood's convict in *The Petrified Forest*. Talking out of the side of his mouth, wearing a day-old beard and a felt hat with the brim turned down, the smiling, tailored youth changed into the shady figure he was to repeat, in many variations, throughout his career. In 1936 Leslie Howard, the star of the play, insisted Bogart duplicate his part on screen, and thus one of the lasting icons of American movies was launched.

Between 1936 and 1941, Bogart made twenty-eight pictures for Warner Bros., but he wasn't a star until he was given a script by W. R. Burnett and a young John Huston. In *High Sierra* (1941), Bogart played a gangster with soul—he got the audience to root for the bad guy. Later that year Huston directed him as icy Sam Spade in *The Maltese Falcon*, and in 1943, on one of the most chaotic movie sets of its era, with scenes whizzing out of typewriters just as the day's filming began and an ending that had yet to be settled on, Bogart had his first romantic role as Rick, the nightclub owner in *Casablanca*. Although he was characteristically humble about the performance ("When the camera moves in on that Bergman's face, and she's saying she loves you, it would make anybody look romantic"), Bogart seemed to have stretched himself. He was nominated for his first Oscar, and he was ready, both in life and on screen, for a new kind of love interest.

He was on his third and most raucous marriage—Dorothy Parker said of the Humphrey Bogart–Mayo Methot ménage that "their neighbors were lulled to sleep by the sounds of breaking china and crashing glass"—when director Howard Hawks told him he was grooming an actress for *To Have and Have Not* who would challenge Bogie's supremacy. "I'm going to try and make a girl as insolent as you are," Hawks said. "Fat chance of that," Bogart retorted. But this was before he met Lauren Bacall. Born Betty Joan Perske in New York, she had done some work at the American Academy of Dramatic Arts, scrabbled for a few small parts on Broadway and floundered as an actress before turning to modeling. Impressed with her looks, Diana Vreeland put her on the cover of *Harper's Bazaar*, where she was noticed by Slim Hawks, the director's wife. "Listen, Sweets, you've always said you can take any girl and make a star of her,"

Slim challenged Hawks, who'd given Rita Hayworth her first break and encouraged Carole Lombard to turn to comedy. Hawks sent for Bacall and put her under contract to him personally. He instructed her to lower her voice and study old Marlene Dietrich movies, and gradually this tentative, nervous Galatea became direct, unflappable, sexy—"steel with curves," as Bogart said later, an ace foil for the older actor. "I just saw your test," he told her when they met for the second time. "We'll have a lot of fun together."

"You don't have to say anything, and you don't have to do anything. Not a thing. Or maybe just whistle. [Pause.] You know how to whistle, don't you, Steve? You just put your lips together and . . . blow." Has a more charged seduction ever been put on film? Bacall the pursuer, Bogart the pursued; offscreen and on, both falling in love. "Baby, I never believed that I could love anyone again," he wrote her. "It was romantic—it was fun—it was exciting—it was all-encompassing," she remembered

"He doesn't build barbeques or stone walls and he has no recipe for spaghetti," Bacall said of Bogart (BELOW: in the garden, circa 1948). "We have fun with a capital F."

in her autobiography, *By Myself*. Their romance lasted through the filming of *To Have and Have Not* and, later that year, *The Big Sleep*. There were interruptions as Bogart extricated himself from his decaying marriage, but on May 21, 1945, the two were wed on Louis Bromfield's farm in Ohio. He was forty-six, she twenty-one.

Bogart and Bacall made two more movies together, *Dark Passage* (1947) and *Key Largo* (1948). Bogart went on to extend his range in *The Treasure of the Sierra Madre* (1948); *The African Queen* (1951), in which he won an Oscar for his performance as Charlie Allnut; and *The Caine Mutiny* (1954), which brought him his third nomination. Bacall made fewer movies as she became a mother (a son, Stephen, was born in 1949; a daughter, Leslie, named for Leslie Howard, in 1952) and made a home for her new family. In 1947, after living in the Garden of Allah and then in what Bacall described as a "honeymoon house" in the Hollywood Hills, they acquired a house in Benedict Canyon.

Previously owned by Hedy Lamarr, it consisted of eight rooms, stood on six and a half acres, and had a pool, a picket fence, and eight coops, where the Bogarts kept an ever-expanding population of chickens, roosters, and ducks. With the help of decorator Bill Yates, Bacall did

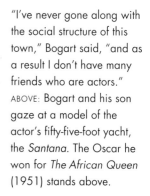

"I've never gone along with the social structure of this town," Bogart said, "and as a result I don't have many friends who are actors." ABOVE: Bogart and his son gaze at a model of the actor's fifty-five-foot yacht, the *Santana*. The Oscar he won for *The African Queen* (1951) stands above.

LEFT: "This is the master's mad room," Bacall said in a 1947 interview, of the plaid-wallpapered room filled with "masculine furnishings" and photographs of the actress. "Anytime he gets peeved or wants to be alone, this is his private sanctum."

most of what *Movieland* called the "interior planning" in a mixture of Dutch, Early American, and French provincial furniture. "Naturally Betty is intensely proud of her achievements . . . , and she has a right to be," the magazine reported. "It's the kind of home where you can be at ease . . . a perfect background for two very likeable people."

Humphrey Bogart and Lauren Bacall seem to have had one of the happiest unions in a town where disheveled marriages, as Bogart's own history demonstrates, are not uncommon. "The remarkable Lauren

Bacall knew who he was, let him be who he was," observed Mary Astor, Bogart's costar in *The Maltese Falcon*. "And, in return, he was at last able to give something no other woman could grab from him: his total commitment." Lauren Bacall recalled of Bogie, "He taught me how to live, that it was okay to trust. He taught me to keep going, no matter what. He did. And he is." They both are. Thanks to the screen's long-term memory, Humphrey Bogart and Lauren Bacall are still a handsome couple: clever, respectful, devoted, sexy—good, awful good.

Cher

At Her Italian Renaissance–Style Refuge on a Malibu Bluff

TEXT BY NANCY COLLINS
PHOTOGRAPHY BY MARY E. NICHOLS

"Every day when I wake up and look out my bedroom window, I'm never not amazed," marvels Cher, staring out one of a myriad of arched windows that define her new house, an Italian Renaissance–style villa that sits high on a bluff, overlooking the Pacific Ocean. "Every room has two views of the ocean, each of which is so beautiful—the water is always glistening, the sunset always happening. My house is so special because it's my sanctuary, my fortress, really—the only place I have any privacy. There's no place else that I would rather be."

Coming from Cher, that says a lot. After all, the singer has turned out a hit—and a house—or two in her time. So when it came to putting together her nineteenth project with designer Ron Wilson she knew what she wanted—and he knew how to make it happen.

"Both structurally and in terms of the interior, this house was Cher's concept," admits Wilson, who worked with project manager Wallace Tutt III and designer

Cher commissioned designer and longtime friend Ron Wilson to decorate an Italian Renaissance–style residence in Malibu. "I'm comfortable here," says the singer-actress (below). "This house wraps its arms around me." LEFT: The rear façade overlooks an infinity-edge pool. "Cher was totally involved with the landscape design, which is unbelievable," says Wilson. "She's very gifted."

ABOVE: "All of the art"—including the circa 1880 oil found in Europe that hangs in the living room—"was of special interest to Cher," says Wilson. "She was responsible for purchasing most of it herself."

LEFT: A late-nineteenth-century painting depicting Jesus Christ and Mary Magdalene, an antique bronze, and a Gothic Revival settle are in the area where the entrance hall meets the lower stair landing. The walls, floors, and staircase, which has an iron balustrade, are stone.

Janet Bussell of Tutt Design Group. "My job is to interpret what she's thinking." It is an enviable marriage of minds that began in Encino, California, when both were teenagers and Wilson drove a slamming Corvette. "She thought I was hot stuff," laughs the designer. "Oh, yeah," concedes the actress, "I had a huge crush on Ronnie."

Until, that is, she met up with a guy called Sonny, with whom she bought her first home: a model house designed by Wilson, who "has worked on every one of my houses since," says Cher. "I've lived through Cher's whole life with her," says Wilson, "and she remembers every second of it."

So it was perhaps not surprising when, inspired by visits to Venice, Cher decided to build her own "version of Venetian" and again turned to Wilson. "Once her mind moved toward Italian Renaissance," says the designer, "she got fifty books and started studying—presenting me with ideas."

RIGHT: In the living room is a Gothic Revival stone mantelpiece that was carved in Mexico. "The house is light," says Cher. "Its walls are light. I don't have a dark wall in the house." Soft velvets and an inlaid-wood low table underscore the interior's muted palette.

LEFT: The gated entrance, and a spacious courtyard beyond, from the private driveway. Wallace Tutt III and designer Janet Bussell of Tutt Design Group contributed to the residence's design.

BELOW LEFT: English bronze chandeliers hang from the dining room's stamped-copper ceiling. Gothic Revival chairs surround a table dressed in silk taffeta and topped with orchids, candlelit centerpieces, and white china with gold trim.

RIGHT: From the loggia is a view of the infinity-edge pool, which seemingly overflows into the Pacific Ocean. An Egyptian sculpture rests on a woven-reed low table. Standing bronze oil lamps are beneath arches supported by columns with vines carved in relief.

"Ron and I work together in a unique way," explains Cher. "I tell him what I want, he says I'm crazy, and then I get it. I bust his chops, but we laugh the whole time."

Three years of laughter later, the Venetian vision à la Malibu became a 16,000-square-foot reality: three stories of bush-hammered travertine, hand-carved marble, stamped-copper ceilings, rugs from Egypt, fireplaces from Mexico, Gothic Revival chandeliers measuring six feet by four feet, a balustrade from San Simeon, and even a tapestry that once hung in the court of Mary, Queen of Scots.

Such attention to detail, of course, doesn't come cheaply, as Cher is the first to admit. Her Italian Renaissance fantasy is a labor of love, financed, she laughs, by her own labors. "My mother once said to me, 'What you need is a very rich man.' And I said, 'Mother, I *am* a very rich man.'"

It is a house as dramatic as its owner. "I like its drama, its splendor," says Cher of the Italian Renaissance sensibility. "It has beautiful pageantry" and strong, definitive lines. "I like very masculine surfaces done in a very feminine way."

"There are two things about this house—and Malibu—that I love," Cher adds. "Malibu is still a village where I know a lot of people and can still walk around as carefree as anyplace I can be in America." And then there's the water. "I love looking at the ocean because there are no boundaries. It doesn't stop anywhere." She pauses. "To me, the ocean is a symbol of infinite possibility." Just like her life.

RIGHT: "The infinity-edge pool is where I spend all of my time in the summer," says Cher. "She's above the beach—a mile from the water," adds Wilson. "Her great love is Malibu." A low, carved marble balustrade defines the outside dining area and grants access to the blue-mosaic-tiled pool.

George Cukor

Sparkling Director of *Holiday, The Philadelphia Story,* and
My Fair Lady

TEXT BY A. SCOTT BERG
PHOTOGRAPHY BY RUSSELL MacMASTERS

George Cukor never forgot his friends. He is usually remembered as the director of Hollywood's most sparkling comedies or as the most lucid interpreter of literary material, even as the man who launched a startling number of important film careers. But anybody who knew him learned quickly that more important than his work were his friendships, which he cultivated to his dying day.

He was born in 1899 in New York to prosperous parents who hoped their only son would become a lawyer. But George—a sadly overweight youth with a hyperactive imagination—announced his intentions of going "into the theater." He spent his twenties learning the ropes—starting as a callboy and quickly rising to become a stage manager, which opened the door to directing. In those salad days he fell in love with a budding actress named Frances Howard; she remained his lifelong friend even after she married Samuel Goldwyn. He was soon directing the likes of Laurette Taylor and Ethel Barrymore—though in later years, Cukor would dismiss his work with the latter as nothing more than planting her

liquor bottles in strategic locations on the set, so that she could secretly "nip her way through a performance."

When talking pictures came in, Hollywood began importing New York stage directors, and Cukor marched to the fore. He began in 1929 as a dialogue director and within a year was directing his first important picture, *The Royal Family of Broadway,* a lampoon of his friends the Barrymores. A new friend, David O. Selznick, signed Cukor to RKO Studios. Tellingly, the director worked with his friends repeatedly—with Selznick more than six times.

Their second collaboration was *A Bill of Divorcement* with John Barrymore; debuting as the ingenue was Katharine Hepburn, who later credited Cukor for much of her success because of the way he "presented" her. The following year he directed her in *Little Women* and earned his first Academy Award nomination.

Over the next decade he worked almost exclusively for MGM, directing *David Copperfield* in 1935, *Romeo and Juliet* and *Camille* with Garbo in 1936. He directed Garbo again in 1941 in *Two-Faced Woman,* her last screen appearance. He guided Ingrid Bergman toward her Academy Award in *Gaslight* and Judy Holliday to hers in *Born Yesterday,* for which Cukor was nominated for another Oscar.

But the actress most closely associated with Cukor was Katharine Hepburn. In nine pictures, their dueling wits sparked movie magic. The first of their comedies was *Holiday* in 1938. They reteamed two years later, uncorking what still stands as the Dom Pérignon of

OPPOSITE: Canvas-cushioned furniture surrounded the swimming pool, where the director, who won an Academy Award for Best Director for *My Fair Lady* (1964), sometimes read scripts.

LEFT: "The best times in my life I remember having here—in my own house," said director George Cukor, who lived in a house not far from the Sunset Strip in Beverly Hills. "It's been an intimate part of my life, my work, my friends—a great many friends."

motion pictures, *The Philadelphia Story*, for which Cukor received another Oscar nomination. No wonder he became known as Hollywood's great "woman's director."

"Oh yes, I'm the great woman's director," Cukor would retort, finding the compliment left-handed. "I've directed John Barrymore, Spencer Tracy, Cary Grant, Laurence Olivier, and Jimmy Stewart." Also Charles Boyer, Melvyn Douglas, Jack Lemmon, James Mason, and Ronald Colman, whose work in *A Double Life* won an Oscar and helped earn yet another nomination for Cukor. Whoever the actor, Cukor's films were marked by unusual energy, sensitivity mixed with vigor. His watchwords on every set were, "Fine, now do it faster."

In 1935 Cukor rebuilt a house he had bought just above the Sunset Strip. From the street, a visitor could see nothing but an uninviting wall with a box containing a telephone. After being buzzed inside, one entered a Cukor production—a house that stood high like a villa on the Côte d'Azur, surrounded by statuary, beautiful gardens, an Olympian pool, and trickling fountains. "It all looks," he said, "just like a Hollywood director's house ought to look."

The interior was a monument to his friends. A bronze bust of Tallulah Bankhead sat on an inlaid table in the downstairs hall. A large, parquet-floored oval room, whose walls held works by Georges Braque and Juan Gris, was often the gathering place for Christopher Isherwood, Aldous Huxley, Thomas Mann, and Somerset Maugham. In the drawing room, he sat Vivien Leigh in a Régence fauteuil and rehearsed her for *Gone With the Wind*, even after he had been fired from the picture. In the dining room—velvet and Venetian—gathered the likes of Ruth Gordon and Garson Kanin and Anita Loos and movie stars of every vintage, newcomers sitting close to the host at the head of the table.

ABOVE: Italian stone statues beckon guests to a belvedere.

"I was a New Yorker and came here with the talkies," Cukor said in 1978, when his house was first featured in *Architectural Digest*. "It never occurred to me that I could live in California. Now I can't imagine living anywhere else." LEFT: Cukor rebuilt the house in 1935.

ABOVE: A pair of Louis XVI bronze sconces in the entrance hall illuminate a suite of antique carved and silvered-wood grotto furniture discovered in Wales.

RIGHT: In the book-lined library, a lamp, whose base is a seventeenth-century carved-wood Kuan-Yin figure, illuminates autographed photographs of President and Mrs. John F. Kennedy, and of Katharine Hepburn and Sir Laurence Olivier.

The part of the house that most intrigued first-time visitors was the hall, which was covered with gratefully inscribed photographs of Cukor's friends—Noël Coward, the Gish sisters, Arthur Rubinstein, Gladys Cooper, Kate, Marilyn, Ingrid, Sophia, Ava. . . .

His career never let up, and when Jack Warner bought the rights to *My Fair Lady*, George Cukor was the obvious choice to direct it. Cukor received his fifth Academy Award nomination thirty-five years after coming to Hollywood. And on Oscar night, Joan Crawford (whom he had directed three times) had the honor of pronouncing him the winner. The overwhelming applause from the crowd indicated it was an overdue award for an entire superior career.

Cukor continued to direct for another fifteen years, right up to his death in 1983. And though his first friend in the theater, Frances Howard, remained married to Samuel Goldwyn for almost fifty years, the two conspired to be buried next to each other, which they are.

"Friendships are of enormous importance to me," Cukor said. ABOVE: A hall lined with photographs of friends.

BELOW: Figures of Katharine Hepburn and Spencer Tracy were displayed against an early-nineteenth-century puppet theater.

LEFT: A bronze head of Tallulah Bankhead rests on an inlaid demilune table in the lower hall.

BELOW LEFT: An elaborate velvet drapery treatment, Neoclassical architectural details, and Venetian parcel-gilt blackamoors combine to create an appropriately theatrical dining room setting. A Victorian épergne stands in the center of the Sheraton pedestal table. "The regulars would sit at the end of the table," the genial director recalled of Hollywood's halcyon years, "and when I had new people, they sat close to me."

BELOW RIGHT: A John Piper watercolor, a painting by Kaminski, and a Vuillard lithograph enrich a large guest room.

"The rooms are more or less the way they were when William Haines decorated them [in the 1930s]," said Cukor. "The house suits me perfectly, and I know that I belong here."

ABOVE: Chinese Chippendale mirrors were mounted over Regency chinoiserie commodes in the drawing room, which was distinguished by elaborate architectural details. Régence fauteuils were covered with Aubusson tapestry.

In Hollywood's halcyon days, after six-day workweeks, the director would host Sunday luncheons at his house. "I don't know how I managed it," he recalled. "There were regulars like Katharine Hepburn and Irene Selznick and Vivien Leigh. Through the years, particularly during the war years, everyone seemed to come here."

RIGHT: Works by, from left to right, John Ferren, Georges Braque, and Juan Gris were displayed in Cukor's oval room, which had a copper fireplace and a parquet floor.

Cecil B. DeMille

Hollywood Residence of a Master Showman

TEXT BY MICHAEL WEBB
PHOTOGRAPHY BY MARY E. NICHOLS

"Produced and directed by Cecil B. DeMille" was, for much of this century, shorthand for extravagance on the screen. DeMille put Hollywood on the map and launched what became Paramount Pictures with a Western, *The Squaw Man*, which he made in the winter of 1913–14. Over the next forty years he directed seventy pictures. Only a handful were biblical epics, but those are the titles for which he is best remembered: *The Ten Com-* *mandments* (1923, 1956), *King of Kings* (1927), *The Sign of the Cross* (1932), and *Samson and Delilah* (1949). DeMille was a master showman in the Barnum and Bailey tradition, and it's appropriate that he won the Best Picture Oscar in 1952 for a circus drama, *The Greatest Show on Earth*.

On the set he acted his role with gusto. Publicity films capture an imperious figure with a hawklike profile and commanding voice, attended by acolytes who relayed his

OPPOSITE: "Keeping the same house for four decades must be something of a record in Los Angeles," Cecil B. DeMille wrote of his Mediterranean-style house in Laughlin Park, which he bought in 1916.

LEFT: DeMille with his granddaughter, Cecilia, circa 1946.

orders to the Crusaders storming Jerusalem or to the Israelites fleeing the pharaoh across the parted Red Sea. A deeply religious man, DeMille believed that every picture must have a moral, and that sin should be exposed in order to extol virtue. This principle allowed him to feature pagan orgies and nude bathing sequences without complaint from the censors. Critics scoffed, but audiences loved it.

DeMille's special brand of uplift and entertainment is out of fashion today, and his films are seldom shown. But he was a towering figure in an era when moguls and stars flaunted their success. Not so DeMille. "Since I came to California in 1913, I have never lived anywhere but Hollywood," he wrote in his autobiography. "We have never been lured by Beverly Hills, Bel-Air, or other places which have become much more fashionable." And the conservative house in which DeMille lived until his death in 1959 suggests a banker or a bishop more than a movie legend.

A prospectus of 1915 described the Laughlin Park subdivision, just south of Griffith Park, as "a residential paradise on a noble eminence, a replica of Italy's finest landscape gardening linked to the city by a perfect auto road." To launch the venture, two substantial classically inspired houses were built side by side: DeMille moved into one with his family; Charlie Chaplin, who became a close friend, took the other. When Chaplin moved out of his Hollywood house in 1926, DeMille bought the property and commissioned architect Julia Morgan to design a conservatory to link the houses.

DeMille came to Hollywood by chance. He had planned to make *The Squaw Man* in Arizona, but when the company reached Flagstaff he realized that the scenery was inappropriate for a Western set in Wyoming. He cabled to New York ("Have rented barn in place called Hollywood for $75 a week") and was given permission to stay.

The "movies," as the pioneers were called, were mostly young and uninhibited. Cowboys hired for Westerns would gallop across neighborhood front lawns.

RIGHT: Among the memorabilia in his office was a Pathé camera that was used to film his first Hollywood feature, *The Squaw Man*, in 1914. Constance DeMille gave her husband the opium bowl, foreground, to remind him not to drop pipe ashes on the carpet.

In addition to his Best Picture Academy Award for *The Greatest Show on Earth* (1952), the same year he won the coveted Irving B. Thalberg Award, DeMille received a nomination for *The Ten Commandments* (1956).

ABOVE: In the living room, the DeMilles entertained notables of the motion picture industry and the diplomatic and theatrical worlds. The painting, *Peasants Listening to the Prayer of a Bishop*, is by Daniel Sayre Groesbeck, associated with DeMille productions for many years.

OPPOSITE: DeMille's Oscar for *The Greatest Show on Earth* was on view in his office at home. In 1913 he cofounded the Lasky company, which became Paramount, and he spent most of his prolific career there. The producer-director-writer is generally credited with helping Hollywood become an important film center.

Producer Mack Sennett staged automobile chases along quiet residential streets, greasing intersections to improve the skids. In many ways this was still the Wild West. Rivals twice tried to shoot DeMille as he rode home to his cottage in the Cahuenga Pass from the barn at Selma and Vine, and he carried a gun to shoot rattlesnakes. Today the barn that served as a set and offices for *The Squaw Man* has been moved to a site across from the Hollywood Bowl, where it displays mementos of those Gold Rush years.

The Squaw Man survived various setbacks and DeMille's inexperience. Its success launched his career, and he used the same camera for good luck when he shot a scene in each of the fifty silent features he made up to the coming of talkies in 1927. DeMille was deeply attached to his past, and his house was a compendium of the man and his career: the books and art that inspired him, the props that recall a half century of moviemaking, a galaxy of awards and citations.

DeMille's granddaughter, Cecilia DeMille Presley, was born and raised there. Her earliest memories are of laughter and of flowers in every room. Halloween was an occasion to dress up in costumes borrowed from the studio wardrobe. Grandfather, an intimidating presence at the studio, was for her a kindly old man who never lost

his patience with children and prowled through the house in the middle of the night to make sure they were well tucked in.

The house was where he entertained heads of state, industry leaders, and military heroes. The rose garden was the setting for family weddings and publicity photos of young actresses: a scene for the 1927 *King of Kings* was shot in the olive grove beyond. Over the years, satellite houses were built on the estate, usurping the pool and stables. W. C. Fields, Deanna Durbin, and Anthony Quinn developed neighboring properties. But the illusion of a sparsely populated arcadia, crowned with the Hollywood sign and the Griffith Observatory, has been preserved.

The office and screening room were DeMille's domain, but it was his wife, Constance, who ran the house and who furnished it with such dignity and restraint. She had met Cecil in the theater, after shocking her proper New England family by deciding to make her career on the stage. As soon as they married, she gave up acting and devoted her life to his welfare, staying up all night if necessary to make cocoa for him when he returned from the studio.

Cecil B. DeMille was too canny a showman to be taken in by his own hyperbole; throughout his life he moved gracefully from directing casts of thousands to the

quieter pleasures of family and friends. Not everyone understood the distinction between the public and the private man. Most DeMille films boasted a risqué bathtub sequence; Gloria Swanson's career was enhanced by her tasteful disrobings; Claudette Colbert bathed luxuriously in a vast pool of asses' milk (which curdled on the second day). Décor achieved dizzy heights as DeMille voyaged back in time. But to the disappointment of credulous visitors, there were no marble nymphs or gold fittings in his own baths.

RIGHT: DeMille bought Charlie Chaplin's house next door to use as an office, screening room, and guesthouse. Linked by a conservatory, the houses enclose a garden often used for publicity stills for his films.

ABOVE: Mrs. DeMille's office and library opened to the music room. The picture of her husband was taken in 1916, the year they bought the house, when he was thirty-five and an increasingly active and significant figure in the burgeoning motion picture industry. The photograph on the bookcase is of DeMille's mother, Beatrice.

OPPOSITE: "I like to paint on a big canvas," DeMille said of his film productions. By contrast, the family's home life was relatively simple, and dinner parties tended to be small and select.

Clark Gable and Carole Lombard

A California Ranch House for the Stars of *Gone With the Wind* and *Nothing Sacred*

BY CHARLES LOCKWOOD

The couple (ABOVE, circa 1940) enjoyed the rural life on the ranch they bought in 1939—Gable driving his tractor and Lombard gathering eggs in the henhouse.

As stars of the silent film era like Mary Pickford, Douglas Fairbanks, Sr., and Harold Lloyd faded into obscurity in the 1930s after the advent of the talkies, so did the notion that actors and actresses must create flamboyant estates to serve as symbols of their success. The new stars of the 1930s—among them Katharine Hepburn, Gary Cooper, Ronald Colman, Joan Crawford, Cary Grant, Bette Davis, and James Stewart—usually lived in handsome but hardly extravagant residences.

Few celebrities exemplified the movie community's shift to simpler lifestyles better than Clark Gable and Carole Lombard. Gable had become one of Hollywood's most successful leading men after winning an Academy Award for Best Actor in Frank Capra's *It Happened One Night* (1934), then by starring in *Mutiny on the Bounty* (1935), *San Francisco* (1936), and *Gone With the Wind* (1939). Lombard was a popular leading lady in screwball comedies, who had appeared in films such as *No Man of Her Own* (1932), *Twentieth Century* (1934), *My Man Godfrey* (1936), and *Nothing Sacred* (1937).

Instead of acquiring an impressive estate, the couple moved to a twenty-acre ranch in the sparsely settled San Fernando Valley town of Encino several months after their marriage in 1939. The property, which included a nine-room house, had belonged to director Raoul Walsh and cost $50,000.

At the ranch, Gable and Lombard enjoyed unspoiled country living, far from the tour buses that prowled the streets of Beverly Hills, yet still an easy drive to the studios. To reach the property, they drove through the farmland and small ranches that still characterized the western portion of the San Fernando Valley before World War II. Behind a high fence and an electronically controlled gate, the couple's own property contained acres of citrus groves and fields of oats and alfalfa, stables, a cow barn, and a pigless pigsty.

The ranch house, which Carole Lombard had renovated while Gable worked on *Gone With the Wind*, featured a white-brick-and-wood-frame façade, spacious red-brick terraces, and a gambrel roof.

Inside, the rooms were decorated in the Early American style. The living room had canary yellow carpeting

RIGHT: Clark Gable and Carole Lombard bought the twenty-acre ranch in Encino. The house was later dubbed "House of the Two Gables."

RIGHT: "I've always wanted a place like this," Gable told Lombard. "It will be the first home I've had . . . that I can really call my own. Ma, I think we're going to be very happy here."

814—Ranch Home of Clark Gable, Encino, California

and white-painted pine paneling, and was comfortably furnished with Early American–style sofas, quilted wing chairs, green club chairs, and a variety of pine tables. The sofas and chairs were oversize to accommodate Clark Gable's large frame. One first-floor bedroom served as his office; another contained his growing collection of firearms.

The second floor comprised two adjoining master suites—his decorated in brown and beige, and hers in blue and white. Aside from the large his-and-hers dressing rooms, the only obvious sign of Hollywood stardom was Carole Lombard's lavish bath, which featured white-marble walls, wraparound mirrors, and crystal and silver fixtures.

Gable and Lombard truly enjoyed their seclusion and country lifestyle. Yet they also knew how to make use of the ranch to enhance Gable's down-home image. Studio publicists photographed him mending fences or driving his tractor around the property. During interviews, he often went to the barn with reporters and milked a cow, or helped Lombard gather eggs in the henhouse. For a while, they even discussed the possibility of getting more chickens and selling "The King's Eggs."

Gable and Lombard's idyllic marriage was sadly short-lived. In 1942 Carole Lombard died in a plane crash as she returned home from a war-bond tour. Grief-stricken, Clark Gable enlisted in the air force, and didn't return home to the Encino ranch until his 1944 discharge.

Gable subsequently remarried, but the ranch complemented his personality so genuinely that he lived there until his own death in 1960. In 1973 his widow, Kay Spreckels Gable, sold the property. By then, Los Angeles had completely engulfed the once-rural area, and though the house survived, the ranch was subdivided into an expensive housing development called the Gable Estates.

RIGHT: Not long after the couple moved into the brick-and-frame house, Lombard began decorating in the Early American style, while Gable continued shooting *Gone With the Wind*.

Greta Garbo

The Legendary Star's Secret Garden in New York

BY GRAY HORAN

"There will never be another Garbo." She said it herself in her own confident, charming manner. She was responding to a magazine article I had shown her about a new actress who was touted as "the next Garbo." "No, there will never be another Garbo," she continued. "I'm different inside." The emphasis was on the last word.

What was she like inside? So few people really knew. Both on and offscreen, Greta Garbo evoked a sense of wonder. She created some of the screen's great characters in movies of the same name: *Queen Christina* (1933), *Anna Karenina* (1935), *Camille* (1936), *Ninotchka* (1939)—all were provocative and timeless. About herself, she left the public guessing. She was determined to live privately.

This was difficult for Garbo. Her beauty and mesmerizing film performances had catapulted her to fame at the cusp of womanhood. She was only seventeen when she starred in Mauritz Stiller's *Gösta Berling's Saga* (1924). With her unparalleled success came the less desirable trappings of stardom. She was pursued throughout her life by persistent fans, reporters, and photographers. She rebelled at the intrusions, wishing desperately to be left alone.

"I was on the lam," Garbo said (she frequently peppered her speech with such colloquialisms), recalling the Hollywood days when she rented or owned a series of houses, constantly moving to elude inquisitive neighbors and relentless voyeurs. When preparing for a role, she was serious and concentrated; she would take her tape recorder to her bedroom and work for hours on end. It left her little time for homemaking. In fact, she acquired relatively few possessions for her home during this period in her life—notably a coveted seventeenth-century Swedish country table that belonged to her beloved film director, Mauritz Stiller, a bedroom set, and a plethora of books on art and history. Of her spartan surroundings Garbo would explain, "I worked. When was I going to sit in the living room?"

Residential Los Angeles offered an unprotected lifestyle. One night the actress found herself dangling from the drainpipe outside of her bedroom window, waiting for the prowler inside to finish prowling. She needed security. It was time to move to New York, which offered both anonymity and doormen. Finally, she would settle down to a place she called home.

In 1953 Garbo bought the fifth-floor apartment at 450 East 52nd Street. Built in 1927 and boasting a Venetian-Gothic façade, it was a site of considerable intrigue, even before Garbo moved in. During Prohibition it housed a private speakeasy called The Mayfair. Situated at the end of a rare Manhattan cul-de-sac, with an unobstructed vista up and down the East River, the building had long had a colorful array of residents. Henry and Clare Boothe Luce maintained a triplex. Noël Coward, Edgar Kaufman, and Alexander Woollcott were also among the illustrious that had made it their home. Though officially called the Campanile, it was dubbed Wit's End by Dorothy Parker. Tickled by the legacy, Garbo moved in.

Collecting paintings, antiques, and furnishings for her new residence became a lifelong, international pursuit. Whether on a "trot" about New York, a brisk walk through Paris, or a cruise around the Mediterranean, Garbo loved the quest for her treasures. What she

OPPOSITE: Renoir's 1909 *Léontine et Coco*, which depicts the artist's son, Claude, is displayed in the living room. Garbo had a passion for art and antiques and began collecting works by Renoir in the 1940s. Louis XV fauteuils attributed to Jean-Baptiste Tilliard flank the fireplace, where late-eighteenth-century famille-rose roosters are set alongside nineteenth-century Chinese porcelain boxes. The taboret is Louis XVI.

ABOVE: David Levine's *The Pink Hat* is one of the paintings in the living room. A friend of the artist's recalls Garbo at the opening in which the seascape was exhibited. "She came in, spotted the painting, bought it, and left—five minutes later."

acquired echoed her inner aesthetic. Her apartment was a place of beauty, wit, and color.

A friend of Garbo's who herself presides over one of the world's greatest private art collections said it best: "She had a natural taste." Although she was fond of discussing art and design with the experts and trendsetters of the day, Garbo had her own instincts. She never followed fashions, she created them. She had tremendous faith in her judgment and was very sure of her innate and diverse talents. "I never set out to be an actress," she once remarked. "I would have been good at a number of things."

Garbo created many colorful rugs for the apartment. The first series she called *Birds in Flight*, which chronicles a particular period in her aesthetic life. She began the series in 1962 with two rugs, one for her bedroom and one for what she called her "closet room," which she had transformed from a small library. The designs are boldly geometric and charged with color. Each has a central medallion motif, and the forms, though abstract, are translatable to their winged inspiration. By 1966, when Garbo made the last rug in this series, the geometric shapes, which she had conceived and sketched, could certainly have been considered avant-garde. The series, though colorful and modern, never compromised her classical sensibilities.

For the halls, Garbo designed runners with a trellis-like pattern. Except for the rugs, the long corridors were relatively unadorned, compared with the rest of the apartment. The flocked brown wallpaper there might have fooled a visitor into expecting musty high Victoriana. In contrast, the chartreuse and shocking-pink tones of her rugs were more suggestive of the gardenlike rooms beyond—her prelude, so to speak. It was all very schematic, though it did not appear to be contrived.

Composing the rugs was a wonderful outlet for Garbo's creativity. She was tireless, involved in every process. Ever practical, she would sit cross-legged on the floor when working on them. To her, it was the obvious perspective from which to design a rug. Roger McDonald, then a young man at V'Soske, the company that produced her designs, recalls his illustrious client: "We worked and we worked until we achieved what *she* wanted." Now V'Soske's design director, McDonald still feels Garbo's influence, particularly with color. "She knew just how to use color to energize a space," he says. "The rugs she designed held to the floor; they were never mincing, never overpowering."

For her bedroom, Garbo disassembled an old Swedish *skåp*, a huge armoirelike piece she had bought many years before at an auction in Stockholm. Typical of her taste in such furnishings, the floral carvings are natural and

OPPOSITE: Pierre Bonnard's *Les Coquelicots* hangs prominently in the living room. Elsewhere are portraits and a still life by Alexej von Jawlensky and oils by Georges Rouault and Juliette Juvin.

BELOW: A carpet Garbo designed lines a hall, where a painting by her brother, Sven Gustafson, hangs above a Louis XV banquette. In the elevator vestibule at right is a circa 1700 British School oil.

ABOVE: Greta Garbo, who created memorable roles in *Anna Christie, Anna Karenina,* and *Ninotchka,* found refuge from the intrusions of an avid public in a New York apartment near the East River from 1953 to her death in 1990.

ABOVE: A panel painted after François Boucher adorns the upper part of a Louis XVI trumeau in the living room. The painted and parcel-gilt demilune commode below is Italian. At right are flower paintings by, from top, Georges d'Espagnat, Kees van Dongen, and Louis Valtat.

RIGHT: Garbo in the jeweled cap she wore in *Mata Hari* (1932). The three-time nominee was given a 1954 Honorary Award for her "unforgettable screen performances"—thirteen years after appearing in her last film.

delicate. After she had the entire piece taken apart, she designed both a bed and a niche with the splendid panels.

For the bedroom and the "closet room," she chose a Fortuny fabric with African tribal symbols set against a mottled salmon-colored background. Despite its primitive roots, the fabric is wonderfully modern.

Garbo was passionate about color. She would frequently proclaim, "Color makes a room sing." Her rooms certainly did. She amassed a collection of hundreds of paintings and artifacts that resonated with color and character. When she spied something in a shop or auction house that struck a chord, she would moan in her deep, wistful voice, "If only I had the room." She learned to find places. In the living room, she hung a veritable chorus of paintings, stacked on the walls up to the ceiling. The bookcases and tables brimmed with whimsical porcelains. The effect was dazzling, like a garden in full bloom.

The apartment was resplendent with flowers, both real and re-created, since her collection was filled with floral motifs. There were delicately carved roses on an eighteenth-century *marquise*; painted tulips decorated a Rococo chest of drawers; the halls were flecked with light from floriated pastel-colored porcelains mounted on small chandeliers. Her art collection included dozens and dozens of splendid and lively floral still lifes by an assortment of artists: Pierre Bonnard, Kees van Dongen, Louis Valtat, Georges d'Espagnat, Alexej von Jawlensky, Madelaine Lemaire, and even Garbo's own artist brother, Sven Gustafson. She was always finding a spot for seductive little anonymous painted bouquets she came across in her travels.

Her selections were not limited to floral subjects, though one might conclude that Garbo was drawn to images of innocence. The Renoir above the fireplace depicted a touching scene of a young nursemaid reading to a boy, the artist's youngest son. Next to it was a small, quiet canvas that might be Garbo herself, seen from behind, staring into a calm sea, wearing a trademark floppy hat.

The actress was credited by her art-collecting contemporaries with acquiring the work of the German Expressionist Jawlensky before it was widely sought after. Her paintings, now known as the Garbo Jawlenskys, were composed between 1915 and 1918. The period is recognized as a time of renewed energy, hope, and

OPPOSITE: Renoir's *Enfant Assis en Robe Bleu (Portrait of Edmond Renoir, Jr.)*, which dates from 1889, hangs above a Régence parquetry commode in the living room. The circa 1835 Staffordshire equestrian figures stand alongside one of a pair of Han pottery vases mounted as lamps. The corner chair is Louis XV.

harmony for the artist. Garbo was fascinated by these paintings, particularly the thickly outlined faces. Jawlensky's portraits are dramatic and bold, color infusing them with a rich poignancy.

Garbo's largest painting, Robert Delaunay's *Woman With Parasol*, was also her favorite. Her eyes would linger over the canvas more than over any other. It featured the artist's wife, Sonia, strolling on a still-moist garden path, a sun shower of vibrant hues.

There were many truly exceptional works in Garbo's collection—paintings of flowers, clowns, children, funny little dogs, and festive people. To her, each had its own story, its own life. Her art provided a colorful audience with which to enjoy the sweeping views from her apartment. And we did—especially at sunset, when the dancing light that reflected off the river below made the apartment a magical place. Shrouded in secrecy, she tended an oasis of color and imagination in the middle of Manhattan. This was Garbo's secret garden.

Judy Garland

The Wizard of Oz Star in Bel-Air

BY GERALD CLARKE

LEFT: At the same time that Judy Garland was making *The Wizard of Oz*, a film that would establish her as a compelling screen presence at the age of seventeen, she and her mother were planning a sprawling house for themselves in Bel-Air.

Maria Callas, who knew about such things, said that the lady had the most superb voice she had ever heard. Bing Crosby, who was also something of an expert, said that when she was in form, no other singer could be compared to her. But Judy Garland was more than a singer, more than an actress, more than a movie star: she was probably the greatest American entertainer of the twentieth century.

She had an early start, and she could scarcely remember a time when she was not on stage. Her parents were both professional performers. Frank Gumm had been singing since he was a boy in Tennessee, and his wife, Ethel, had been playing the piano since she was a girl in Michigan. After they married in 1914 and settled down in Grand Rapids, Minnesota, they continued to perform at Frank's movie house, providing a live addition to the silent films.

As their three daughters came along, they were also inducted, one by one, into the act. Judy, born Frances, who was the youngest, made her debut at Christmastime 1924. She was just two and a half when she belted out the words to "Jingle Bells"—over and over again—until her father finally pulled her off the stage. The applause thrilled her, and she was hooked on it for life. There is nothing so exciting, she would later say, as the sound of clapping hands.

LEFT AND OPPOSITE: In the backyard of her dream home, late 1939. Behind and alongside the home, there were both tennis and badminton courts, a solarium, and a garden pool and walkway.

848—Residence of Judy Garland, Bel Air, California

OB-H506

LEFT: Postcards that depicted "the homes of the stars!" were a Hollywood tourist staple. After their divorces and prior to their second marriages, both of Garland's older sisters also lived in the house at varying times.

In 1926 the family moved west. Frank and Ethel had hoped to buy a movie house in Los Angeles, but they had to settle for one in Lancaster, two and a half hours away in the Mojave Desert. By the late 1920s the Gumm sisters had become an act, and Ethel, a tirelessly ambitious stage mother, toured with them throughout the West and as far east as Chicago, where they sang at the World's Fair in 1934. According to Garland, the theater in which they were performing had inadvertently spotlighted them as "the Glum Sisters," and comedian George Jessel, who was on the same bill, suggested that they drop Gumm—which, he quipped, rhymed with words like *crumb* and *dumb*—in favor of Garland. Little Frances came up with Judy on her own. From then on she was Judy Garland.

Like a thousand other stage mothers, Ethel Gumm had been pounding on studio doors for years. At last, in September 1935, her efforts paid off when Judy, who was the real star of the Garland trio, signed a contract with MGM. Judy had everything she—or, at least, her mother—wanted, but happiness crumbled just a few weeks later when her father, whom she worshiped, died suddenly of spinal meningitis. It was a tragedy that shadowed the rest of her life.

Though MGM knew that it had acquired an unusual talent, it had no idea what to do with a chubby thirteen-year-old with a grown-up voice. In fact, Garland did her first feature film, *Pigskin Parade* (1936), on loan to Twentieth Century Fox. MGM never loaned her out again, and during the next couple of years she was given increasingly important roles in such pictures as *Thoroughbreds Don't Cry* (1937)—the first of the many films she made with Mickey Rooney—*Everybody Sing* (1938) and *Listen, Darling* (1938). The picture that made her a star, of course, was *The Wizard of Oz* (1939). To millions all over the world she will be remembered forever as the lovable Dorothy, wistfully searching for happiness somewhere

LEFT: On a rare day off from filmmaking or rehearsals, Garland was often required to pose for the kind of "just folks at home" photos that ran in fan magazines and other publications of the day.

LEFT: Garland's mother threw a huge "tea and cocktail" party at the house on Sunday, June 15, 1941; the occasion commemorated the star's nineteenth birthday five days earlier and served to officially announce her engagement to composer and conductor David Rose, who was twelve years her senior. Among the attendees: Joan Crawford (pictured here with Judy), Lana Turner, James Stewart, Tony Martin, Ann Sothern, George Murphy, and Johnny Mercer.

BELOW: At home, 1940. Photographers would regularly invade the Garland grounds to capture pictures that underscored her "girl next door" image.

over the rainbow. A 1939 special Oscar honored her for her "outstanding performance as a screen juvenile."

It was during the making of the picture that Garland and her mother planned their new house on one of Bel-Air's most bucolic streets. Though she was still a teenager, Garland was deeply involved in the project, and she probably provided much of its inspiration. During the years in Lancaster her mother had forced her to spend much of her time on the road, going from audition to audition, job to job; later, in Los Angeles, there had been a series of apartments and rented houses. The house in Bel-Air was to be the first permanent home she had had since leaving Minnesota twelve years earlier.

It was thus not just a house but a romantic vision of what home was meant to be. And like the studio art direc-

tors of the '30s and '40s, Garland identified that platonic ideal not with the sun-drenched houses she saw around her in California but rather with the Christmas-card images of New England, where, as everyone who had ever been to the movies knew, there was always snow on the ground for the holidays and, inside, happy families drank hot chocolate around a fire. The Bel-Air house, with its warm brick exterior, its covered front porch, its rustic shingles, and its understated dormers, almost looked as if it had been transported from Connecticut.

The interior was decorated by Mabel Cooper, the mother of another famous child star, Jackie Cooper, and it was everything a teenage girl could want. Garland had her own suite on the second floor, with a private bath, a dressing room, and a spacious bedroom. It was there that

ABOVE: The mirrored dressing room.

OPPOSITE: Her master suite included a then-state-of-the-art home recording machine and was decorated with photographs of Garland's family and treasured coworkers.

she often entertained her friends, boys as well as girls, listening to records and talking about the studio—they were, after all, all movie kids.

Ironically, Garland's new home was no more permanent than any other she had lived in. On June 15, 1941, her mother set up yellow beach umbrellas on the back lawn, and before six hundred guests she announced Garland's engagement to composer and conductor David Rose, the first of her five husbands. Bride and groom soon found a residence of their own.

The rest of the Garland story is one of great success and great failure. She went on to make some of the most glorious musicals in film history, from *Meet Me in St. Louis* (1944), directed by her second husband, Vincente Minnelli, and *Easter Parade* (1948) to *A Star Is Born* (1954), for which she was nominated for Best Actress.

(She also received a Best Supporting Actress nomination for her performance in 1961's *Judgment at Nuremberg*.) But she was plagued by emotional problems and an addiction to prescription pills, and her failure to report to work caused MGM to fire her in 1950. A year later she emerged into bright sunlight with a sensational concert at the Palladium in London. Such ups and downs continued until her death in London on June 22, 1969, the result of an accidental overdose of drugs. She had just turned forty-seven.

ABOVE: In her suite, 1939. "She was a great reader," admired Garland's later London publicist Matthew West. "Books were everywhere."

OPPOSITE: With oldest sister Mary Jane (Susie) Gumm, an unidentified friend, and Mickey Rooney, Christmas 1939. The holidays capped Garland's most successful year to date. For the first time, Garland ranked among the top ten box office stars. In October, she'd placed her hand and footprints in the cement at Grauman's Chinese Theatre; two months after this picture was taken, Rooney would present her with her special Academy Award.

Cary Grant and Randolph Scott

The Debonair Leading Man and the Western Star in Santa Monica

BY GERALD CLARKE

"Easy to live with, considerate of others, doesn't interfere or try to give advice however well meant." As if that were not encomium enough, his friend, said Randolph Scott, was also a graceful winner and a good loser, a man with a "punchy sense of humor." With that catalogue of virtues, who could ask for anything more in a housemate? Scott certainly couldn't, and in a town where marriages often lasted no longer than the cycles of the moon, his relationship with Cary Grant was a model of permanence and stability. On and off for a decade, from 1932 to 1942, the two actors shared apartments and houses, a convenient arrangement that was interrupted when one or the other got married, then resumed when both were free, as they most often were, because of separation or divorce. "Here we are," Grant explained to a fan magazine, "living as we want to as bachelors with a nice home at a comparatively small cost."

When they met at Paramount in 1932, they were both relatively low-paid contract players with promising but uncertain futures. A onetime acrobat and tumbler, Grant still carried both the name, Archibald Leach, and the accent he had brought from England twelve years earlier. A former University of North Carolina football player, the Virginia-born Scott still sounded like a true son of the Confederacy and still looked as if he could score a touchdown for the Tar Heels.

"You big beautiful American!" exclaims Ginger Rogers, giving him a gander in the musical *Roberta* (1935). Immediate friends, the big beautiful American and the big beautiful Englishman were soon living together in a Hollywood Hills house (dubbed Bachelors' Hall by Carole Lombard), just below Griffith Park and not far from the Paramount lot. "Cary and Randy are really opposite types, and that's why they get along so well," said a reporter who visited them in 1932. "Cary is the gay, impetuous one. Randy is serious, cautious. Cary is temperamental in the sense of being very intense. Randy is calm and quiet. Need I add that all the eligible

Known for his urbane comic flair in *Bringing Up Baby* and *Holiday*, Cary Grant revealed a darker side in later films. "I used to be Noël Coward. Hand-plunged-in-the-pocket," he said. "It took me three long years to get my silly hand out of there." OPPOSITE: Grant, right, and Randolph Scott relax in the living room of the Santa Monica house they rented in the 1930s.

Grant's frugality was well known among his friends. "Cary opened the bills, Randy wrote the checks, and if Cary could talk someone out of a stamp, he mailed them," said Carole Lombard. Playwright Moss Hart once noted that if he stayed with Grant and Scott for more than a few days, they would give him an itemized bill for his laundry, phone calls, and incidentals. RIGHT: Scott, star of *Last of the Mohicans* and *Ride the High County*, with Grant in the study. OPPOSITE: Grant picks out a tune on the piano as Scott stands by. From 1932 to 1942 the actors shared a variety of residences, from a West Hollywood bungalow to a hacienda in the Hollywood Hills. Guests to the beach house included Noël Coward, Dorothy Lamour, and neighbors David Niven and Errol Flynn.

(and a number of the *in*eligible) ladies-about-Hollywood are dying to be dated by these handsome lads?"

The handsome lads seemed to bring each other luck, and their careers quickly soared. Scott was given leads in RKO and Paramount musicals—including *Follow the Fleet* (1936) and *High, Wide and Handsome* (1937)—as well as action adventures like *Last of the Mohicans* (1936).

"Never much on heavy acting," as one film history politely phrased it, he gradually settled into the Western roles for which he was best suited, usually playing straight-shooting lawmen in such sagebrush melodramas as *Abilene Town* (1946), *Albuquerque* (1947), and *Man in the Saddle* (1951). When he finally took off his spurs in 1962, Scott, who died in 1987, had made an even hundred

Wife (1940), in which Grant vied with Scott for the affections of Irene Dunne. (Grant won.)

Learned essays have tried to uncover the secret of his seemingly effortless style of acting, but Grant gave it away for the asking. "The tough thing," he said, "the final thing is to be yourself. That takes doing." But do it he did, so superbly well that it was not until after he retired in 1966 that many people realized that he was one of the greatest actors ever to stand before a camera. The sad fact is that though he made seventy-two movies, Grant, who died in 1986, never won an Oscar for Best Actor, or even Best Supporting Actor. (In 1969 the Academy gave him an Honorary Award.)

Though Grant and Scott shared several addresses, the one most of their friends remembered was the Santa Monica beach house they rented in the mid-1930s. The rear faced the highway and had space for a two-car garage, in which Grant parked his Packard roadster; Scott, his Cadillac. On one side of the house, a walled patio provided privacy and a generous area for trees and greenery. The front faced the ocean and a large pool, giving the living room a sweeping sea view. There was a small dining room, and over the garage was a kind of playroom, with a bar, tables for backgammon, and a piano, on which, as one friend fondly recalled, Grant always seemed to be trying to finish Gershwin's *Rhapsody in Blue*. "As far as I know," she said, "he never made it."

A happy house, it was filled with laughter on weekends, and invitations to Sunday brunch were justly prized. Enjoying the sun and the surf were such guests as Noël Coward, Dorothy Lamour, Hal Roach, Cesar Romero, and Douglas Fairbanks, Jr., along with their assorted wives and girl and boyfriends. David Niven and Errol Flynn, who also shared a beach house—Cirrhosis-by-the-Sea, theirs was called—sometimes dropped in to enjoy the celebrated company. Never far from sight was Grant's four-footed alter ego, a Sealyham terrier he named Archie Leach. Only once, as far as anyone knows, did any visitor fluster the unflappable Grant. "Oh," he said when Greta Garbo came to tea. "I'm so happy you met me." Garbo probably was happy to have met him—everybody else was—and the amiable Scott as well.

The beach house eventually found new tenants, as both men married new wives and formed separate households. But it remains occupied, as it was then, in memories and memoirs, and unlike many movie star residences, which had sad and sometimes tragic histories, the house knew only amusing stories: of spirited Ping-Pong games by the pool, of backgammon in the game room, and of Grant sitting at the piano, struggling—though not too obviously—to finish *Rhapsody in Blue*.

Though he is considered among the finest film actors, Grant never won a competitive Oscar, only an Honorary Award. He kept no photographs of himself in the house except in the bath, which he felt was the only appropriate place for them. Scott, who played mostly romantic leads before turning to Westerns in the late 1930s, made a hundred movies. ABOVE: Grant and Scott rarely used the living room, instead preferring the playroom, which ran the width of the house and overlooked the pool.

pictures and, thanks to his invariably sunny disposition, many more friends. "One of the finest men in Hollywood," observed Dorothy Lamour, one of his early costars. "Always the Southern gentleman," declared Fred Astaire, who affectionately nicknamed him the Sheriff.

Grant's stardom was of a far brighter magnitude. "I think he is the most charming man who ever appeared on the screen," said Joan Crawford, and for sixty years audiences have happily agreed. Mae West was perhaps the first to grasp that a sly sex appeal went along with the charm, and she cast him opposite her in *She Done Him Wrong* and *I'm No Angel*, both in 1933. From then on he needed no help, and a list of his pictures reads like a guidebook of Hollywood landmarks: *Topper* (1937), *Bringing Up Baby* (1938), *Gunga Din* (1939), *The Philadelphia Story* (1940), *Suspicion* (1941), *Notorious* (1946), *To Catch a Thief* (1955), *An Affair to Remember* (1957), and *North by Northwest* (1959). Not the least of his films was Garson Kanin's delightful screwball comedy *My Favorite*

"Each of us is dying for affection," Grant once said. "That's why I became an actor. I was longing for affection. I wanted people to like me."

"Cary will never know peace as long as his name spells news," Scott would say of his roommate.
ABOVE: The actors in the dining room. They became

friends in 1932 on the set of *Hot Saturday* and went on to appear together, eight years later, in the comedy *My Favorite Wife*, with Irene Dunne.

Jean Harlow

The Star of *Dinner at Eight* and *Bombshell* in Holmby Hills

BY DAVID STENN

By the fall of 1932, twenty-one-year-old Jean Harlow was the most famous blonde in films—and the most infamous. That Labor Day her second husband, MGM executive Paul Bern, had stripped naked, stood before a mirror, put a gun to his temple, and pulled the trigger. The ensuing scandal (besides being impotent, Bern was a bigamist whose common-law wife committed suicide the day after his death) seemed to fit Harlow's screen image: an amoral slut who drove men to their doom.

Actually, she was the antithesis of this. Born in 1911 to a Kansas City dentist and his domineering wife, she had been christened Harlean Carpenter and doted upon by her mismatched parents. A prototypical "poor little rich girl," towheaded Harlean grew up in a Gillham Road mansion that was staffed by a nanny, a nurse, two housemaids, a houseman, and a liveried chauffeur; her clothes were handmade and her coverlets were ermine. For the rest of her life family and friends called her "the Baby";

as Harlean herself later admitted, she did not learn her real name until her first day of school. She was six.

Five years later, "Mother Jean" (as she chose to be called) Carpenter scandalized Kansas City society by divorcing her husband and departing for Hollywood, where she tried in vain to attain film stardom. Lacking any interest in acting, Harlean was sent to Ferry Hall, an exclusive finishing school in Lake Forest, Illinois. On a weekend trip to Chicago she met Charles McGrew, an idly rich playboy who was instantly smitten. In the throes of first love, the couple married in 1927. McGrew was twenty. Harlean was sixteen.

To escape his meddling mother-in-law, her husband took Harlean west and bought a house in Beverly Hills, where the newlyweds lived happily, until Mother Jean and her new husband, unemployed gigolo Marino Bello, showed up in Los Angeles shortly thereafter. With her own dreams of film fame dashed forever,

On the set of *Saratoga* (1937), Harlow explained, "I'm not a great actress, and I never thought I was. But I happen to have something the public likes." OPPOSITE: A star turn by the pool. RIGHT: The star shows off her Cadillac in front of her house in Holmby Hills.

LEFT: Mother Jean bought the furniture for the house, including the dining room's Louis XVI–style suite.

OPPOSITE: A wall of photographs includes one of her sometime costar Clark Gable.

Mother Jean focused all her ambition upon her daughter, who still had no interest in acting. Mother Jean urged her to try anyway, and ever the dutiful daughter, Harlean obeyed. On the obligatory trip to Central Casting, she registered under her mother's maiden name: Jean Harlow.

From the start, striking Jean Harlow stood out in a crowd, so extra work came immediately, followed by bit parts in Laurel and Hardy two-reelers and then, in 1929, the proverbial "discovery," by a twenty-three-year-old Texan financing his own three-million-dollar film, a World War I epic entitled *Hell's Angels.* Hollywood considered him "a country hick" and "the sucker with the money." His name was Howard Hughes.

Released in 1930, *Hell's Angels* introduced a classic come-on—"Would you be shocked if I put on something more comfortable?" its femme fatale asks a future conquest—and turned Jean Harlow into an overnight, international star. Whether or not she could act was beside the point: "It doesn't make much difference what degree of talent she possesses," proclaimed *Variety* of Harlow, "for this girl is the most sensuous figure to get in front of a camera in some time. She'll probably always have to play these kind of roles, but nobody ever starved possessing what she's got."

For two years this forecast seemed true, until Paul Bern brought Harlow to MGM and utilized her heretofore hidden talent: an innate knack for making sex funny. A brilliant new career began in films like *Red Dust* (1932), *Bombshell* (1933), *China Seas* (1935), *Libeled Lady,* and *Suzy* (both 1936), in which Harlow wooed and won, among others, Clark Cable, Cary Grant, Spencer Tracy, and Wallace Beery, who also played her boorish husband in *Dinner at Eight* (1933). Its director, George Cukor, recognized Harlow's comic genius. "She was unique among actresses," Cukor recalled. "She had that rare quality of speaking lines as though she didn't quite understand them." That this "dumb blonde" on-screen was actually an avid reader and well-known wit (Harlow was wed three times by age twenty-two and called these unions "marriages of inconvenience") was ignored in Hollywood, where Harlow was typed as the harlots she played. "They treat me," she sighed to a friend about her "fast" reputation, "like a bitch in heat."

Resenting her stardom, which was her mother's wish, not her own, Harlow drank heavily after Paul Bern's death. Meanwhile, Mother Jean purchased (with her daughter's money) a plot on Beverly Glen and Sunset boulevards in tony Holmby Hills, just outside the bounds of Bel-Air. There she supervised the construction of a two-story, four-bedroom residence that MGM promptly dubbed "the Whitest House in the World." Designed to highlight Harlow's trademark white hair, wardrobe, and film sets, her new house had a Georgian

After starring in such films as *Red-Headed Woman* (1932) and *Bombshell* (1933), Harlow became known as a comedienne as well as a leading lady. Mother Jean supervised the design of her daughter's house. LEFT: The actress poses in the white-satin-and-gilt salon, beside a baby grand, which neither she nor her mother could play.

"I wasn't born an actress, you know," said Jean Harlow to a reporter in a 1937 interview. "Events made me one." RIGHT: Harlow peruses a magazine in her sunroom beside the pool.

façade and French furnishings shielded from the California sunshine by both satin draperies and venetian blinds. Its mantels were marble, its upholstery velvet, and its baby grand piano was painted light green for an off-white, pastel effect. All antiques were bought by Mother Jean, "a pain in the ass" who drove a hard bargain. Other ostentatious touches included a walk-in refrigerator, a polar-bear-skin rug, a gilt Cupid, and ermine-covered toilet seats with tassels. The headboard of Harlow's huge bed was also upholstered in white ermine.

With her $1,500-a-week salary, Harlow could afford such extravagance, but at a time when the average family income was $1,600 per year, her own White House was a source of embarrassment. "She told me she wasn't too crazy about this big house, but her mother and Bello liked it," said fellow MGM actress Anita Page. Heeding her studio's command, Harlow posed in her new residence for photographer George Hurrell; in private, however, she thought the place hilarious. "Get a load of this!" Harlow giggled before showing a guest her white-on-white bedroom. Few visitors saw the adjoining sitting room, which Harlow filled with her favorite books. Few would believe she read them.

By 1935 Harlow's affair with actor William Powell was common knowledge to her fans. A man of the world almost twice her age, Powell thought Harlow's house absurd and urged her to economize before her mother spent all her money. That same year Mother Jean divorced Marino Bello, whose extortionary "settlement" requirement made a change of address not only advisable but necessary. To pay off her ex-stepfather, Harlow sold her home in 1936 for $125,000 and leased a Beverly Hills house for $300 a month. It was a prudent move that came too late: a year later, at age twenty-six, Harlow succumbed to kidney disease.

Nearly seven decades after her death, Jean Harlow's heavily remodeled house still stands. Hidden by a wall and front gates, it remains a reminder of the "Platinum Blonde," a reluctant sex symbol made immortal on film.

RIGHT: A 1930s color postcard depicts Harlow's residence, which MGM called "the Whitest House in the World." Embarrassed by its opulence, she once jokingly referred to the mansion as her "half-paid-for car barn."

Katharine Hepburn

Four-Time Best Actress at Home in Connecticut

BY CYNTHIA MCFADDEN

I'm not good at public life.
—Katharine Hepburn

If she found public life hard, she found home life easy: she adored her homes, decorating them, running them, living in them. Home made sense to her. Hollywood, she said, never did.

There were rules about home: Sheets had to be white. Only white. Flowers had to be cut for every room. She was as happy with a bunch of carnations as she was with her beloved Casablanca lilies. She often kept her flowers in their vases a day or two beyond their natural lives—but she accused anyone who suggested it might be time to throw them away of "not giving the poor things a chance."

In summer, her homes were filled with bunches of wildflowers—often gathered from the side of the highway. On the two-hour drive from her New York town house on 49th Street to her sprawling white-brick

OPPOSITE: "Fenwick is and always has been my . . . paradise," Hepburn said of her family's summer cottage in Connecticut.

LEFT: Katharine Hepburn in a 1933 photograph by Ernest A. Bachrach.

home at Fenwick on Long Island Sound, she traveled with a white plastic wastebasket filled with water and a pair of clippers, just in case something tempting was seen on the way. I often wondered what the truck drivers whizzing by on I-95 thought to see her clipping butterfly weed or Queen Anne's lace on the side of the road.

More rules. The room where she sat had to have a fireplace. It had to burn at night regardless of the weather. If that meant turning on the air-conditioning, so be it. There were even rules about the wood she burned. It should never be purchased. Driftwood, collected oneself, was preferable. Wood one had collected and sawed was also acceptable. Her houses smelled faintly of ashes and flowers.

She had strong views about color. White was good. Furniture slipcovered in white cotton canvas was good—the starting point. Red the accent. But red could be tricky. "Make certain it is Chinese red," I remember her saying, when I called to report having found a cashmere throw I thought she might like. She thought red with too much blue in it was depressing. Yellow was out. Period. "No woman looks good in it or around it."

"Never bring me yellow flowers again," she scoffed more than twenty years ago. Needless to say, I never did. That was it for yellow. I will note that sunflowers seemed to get a special dispensation, for reasons I never dared ask.

Next to color, nothing mattered more than proportion. This was true for rooms and furniture. "What a beautifully proportioned room," was the highest compliment she could give. The translation of this, I came to understand, was that the room in some way resembled her living rooms in Connecticut or New York: very high ceilings and length somewhat greater than width.

She adored antiques. Good ones. She knew the difference. Many a shop owner was astonished to find her under a trestle table checking out the construction or getting a look at the craftsman's mark. She and her father, a well-known Hartford surgeon and urologist, shared a love of well-crafted furniture, and they conspired together to have several pieces made, including her New York dining room chairs, which she declared were "simply perfect." "Men," she said, "are unhappy sitting at a dining room table if their chairs don't have arms." I never argued. Although it is worth pointing

out that she rarely ever dined at her New York dining room table (a gateleg find from a London trip years ago), preferring trays in front of the fire.

Kate often said she was confident that in a past life she had been a "rug merchant." As a result of her past lives, perhaps, most rooms in her houses were the recipients of multiple carpets. Nothing odd there, except that they were laid on top of one another, forming rather an archaeological dig of past travels. She preferred rugs with lots of color and pattern. Her theory: when guests spilled their food, it would not show. Colorful rugs kept a number of her friendships alive.

Her passion for beautiful things in general and beautiful rugs in particular was on full display one dappled February day in Boca Grande, Florida. Kate rented a house in the Gulf Coast enclave for several winters, where she marveled at the distinctive homes of various du Ponts and others, including her own cousin Arthur Houghton and his wife, Nina. This day, however, I had arrived for a visit in time to be told that we were going to lunch at Jane Engelhard's home. Neither of us knew the great philanthropist, collector, and patron of the arts very well. And, Kate worried, "Lady Bird Johnson is coming. Maybe Brooke Astor. You," Kate said, pointing a finger at me, "are to do the talking." We arrived first. Mrs. Engelhard asked if we'd like to look around. We ended up in the master bedroom, standing on an enormous pale rug that stretched from wall to wall. Without hesitation, Kate lay down, face first, spread-eagle, rubbing her hands on the distinctive rug. "Get down here," she commanded. "This is the most sensational Bessarabian rug you are ever going to see. Don't miss the experience." She may have been reluctant to talk, but touching was something else.

ABOVE: Quilted and embroidered pillows line a sunny window seat elsewhere in the room. The house is set on a peninsula that projects into Long Island Sound, and Hepburn often rose early to take a swim—no matter what the weather—when she was up for the weekend. "It's the shock," she once explained of her daily ritual, "so horrible that it makes you feel great afterwards." RIGHT: The actress imprinted her own style on the house, furnishing it with an African chief's chair, one of the many artifacts she brought back from the Congo, where she filmed *The African Queen* (1951).

A note on wear and tear. Kate did not believe in replacing things if they got banged up, chipped, rusted, or somehow "lived life," as she put it. Things were routinely glued or nailed back together or simply allowed to remain "natural" or "ratty," as she called it. She felt that "perfection" was not in having sparkling new items about but in surrounding oneself with things you went through life with. Friends, so to speak. She adored the tables and stools from Africa that she shipped home after *The African Queen*; the goose that hung in New York and that she had once given to Spencer Tracy. I find I know a lot about her things because she enjoyed talking about them: the hats, the tennis racket that Martina gave her, the old skates and skis. Before Ralph Lauren taught America about living "haute WASP," she was old New England: the golf clubs and the lamps made of bowls or baskets she liked, the all-American decoys and eagles.

She adored painters and often said that in her next life she would like to be a painter, "since," as she put it,

LEFT: On her bed are a needlepoint pillow and quilted coverlet. BELOW: A metal-banded barrel bookcase, a pair of carved duck decoys, and a painted side chair are arranged in a sitting area of Hepburn's bedroom, on the waterfront side of the house.

"they get to work alone." Her own paintings, both those she collected and those she painted herself, were prominently featured in both homes. What there never were in the public rooms were photographs. She thought it vulgar. But in her bathroom, there they were. The people she loved and counted on: her mother and father. Spencer. The nieces and nephews and brothers and sisters. And this woman whose own picture had been taken so many times—so beautifully by so many—had no photographs of herself around. "That," she explained, "is the creature. I don't bring her home."

RIGHT: The living room, like many rooms in the house, was characterized by simple, comfortable furniture, the odd collectibles from antique stores, and a large fireplace tended to every night regardless of the weather and often burning with driftwood from the beach nearby.

BELOW: A grouping of rustic bowls and baskets hang in Hepburn's kitchen, typical of her casual style.

Anjelica Huston and Robert Graham

The Artist Sculpts a Venice House for His Actress Wife

TEXT BY JOSEPH GIOVANNINI
PHOTOGRAPHY BY TIM STREET-PORTER

LEFT: Huston in the living room.

Robert Graham's two great loves—Venice, California, and Anjelica Huston—seemed mutually exclusive. Since 1971 the noted Los Angeles sculptor has worked in studios set among the cast-iron arcades of the scruffy, ready-for-anything beach town, just yards from the fire-eaters, chainsaw jugglers, gyroscope surfers, skateboard dancers, and all-around abracadabra men of the boardwalk. Here, poets and muscle men commingle in a republic of free-wheelers that for decades has nurtured many Los Angeles artists who are collected internationally. The woman in Graham's life, however, lived above the city on Mulholland Drive, miles away and a world apart. Would she ever come down from the hill?

They held their wedding reception on a small vacant lot next to his studio, the site of a former bank, where Meryl Streep, Mick Jagger, and Warren Beatty celebrated with Westside artists and architects, including Ed Moses, Tony Berlant and Frank Gehry. But after the festivities and the honeymoon in Oaxaca, living with Huston turned Graham into a reluctant commuter. He joked that for each year of shuttling between the Mulholland house and the Venice studio, he could have spent twenty-seven days on a beach in Hawaii. The couple considered moving and looked at many houses. Nothing married their different worlds.

During their honeymoon they had stayed at the El Presidente, a sixteenth-century convent transformed into a hotel, and it gave them the idea that a courtyard house, even in hyperactive Venice, might make Anjelica feel less exposed. After more fruitless house hunting, the beach town began to make sense: her work didn't tie her to any one place, but his foundry committed him

OPPOSITE: Straddling the bronze courtyard door is a three-ton block of marble. "It's a handmade house with fleshy concrete and rubbed-in, patinated surfaces," Graham notes. "It runs the spectrum of warm to cold, depending on how the light hits it."

to Venice. Besides, Graham owned the nuptial lot, and it was still vacant.

They decided to build a house of their own, and he would play architect to her client. "Creating a house is almost like making a portrait or sculpture—you reflect the person," Graham says. "Sometimes designers can't do it because there is no one to hang the portrait on. But when you have someone like Anjelica, all the lives are there. You color them in."

Anjelica, of course, is the Maerose of *Prizzi's Honor* (1985), Lily of *The Grifters* (1990), Morticia of *The Addams Family* (1991), and Etheline of *The Royal Tenenbaums* (2001), an actor who grew out of her identity as the daughter of the legendary writer-director John Huston and granddaughter of actor Walter Huston into a name of her own.

Robert Graham first became known for his mischievously erotic miniature tableaux—couples caught romping on large beds in small acrylic boxes. He went on to realistic, anatomically detailed bronzes—classical nudes appear airbrushed in comparison done by the lost-wax method and cast by rehabilitated gang members from the neighborhood.

"I built the house for Anjelica," says the sculptor, looking prophetic with his mane of gray hair, "and she's a tough client."

"I told him I like arches, domes, white, and plaster," Huston responds. "I like iridescence, and I like light. I like Mediterranean, balconies, and terra-cotta. I like circular things, I like wood, I like nature, I like farm animals. I like eggs."

"So that's how we started," nods Graham. "The client liked eggs."

The two- and three-story house that Graham designed for his spirited wife stands hard by the street, like a town house. A cobra-shaped cowlick at the parapet rises mysteriously behind a high terra-cotta-colored masonry wall with a three-ton stone wedged over the entrance gate. The solid fence isolates the yard in complete privacy so that visitors stepping through the gate into the garden already feel inside the house. From the outdoor walkway a wide courtyard works as an exterior room and functions as the heartspace of the place, offering elemental pleasures—the shade of a mature coral tree, the stillness of water in a lap pool, and a patch of sky squared off by tall white planes. Patinated walls, troweled

"He gave me a very beautiful shell in which to place my oyster," says Anjelica Huston of her husband, sculptor Robert Graham (top), who designed their Venice, California, house.

ABOVE: A terra-cotta-colored wall contributes to the building's solid massing at the street elevation.

OPPOSITE: A Mexican carved icon stands on a plateau of the living room wall; a pair of giltwood lamps carved as archangels flank the fireplace. "Light is essential to the design," Graham says. "The unpainted plaster actively picks it up, absorbs it, and throws it back."

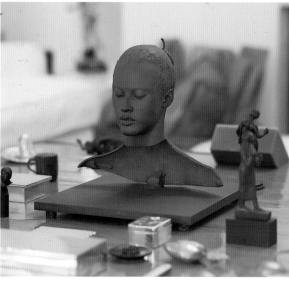

LEFT: A Graham figure fragment, whose base is engraved "For Anjelica" and (twice) "Love," rests on a low table in the living room, surrounded by pieces that include silver temple bells.

"Bob is training me in restraint," says Huston, "but not in austerity or minimalism." ABOVE: In the living room, needlework pillows by Huston's mother are scattered on the sofas. The harlequin tapestry is nineteenth-century French.

OPPOSITE: The Ming-style table and chairs, from the estate of Empress Su Lin, were discovered by Huston in Los Angeles's Chinatown. On the *tansu* chest are a circa 300 A.D. Gandhara head and a silver tray given to John Huston by the cast and crew of *The Asphalt Jungle*. Above is a David Novros oil-on-canvas triptych, 1971.

by hand, and flesh-colored floors give the sense of a structure sensuously crafted. You feel the design on your skin.

It would be easy to think of this courtyard house as Mexican, but Graham, who was born in Mexico, simply reworked an ancient architectural archetype when he devised the plan (the construction documents and general contracting were done by John Cordic) according to his and Huston's needs and the restrictions of the site. The parsimonious fifty-by-one-hundred-foot lot, its location on a brassy street, and the desire for privacy led him to circle rooms around the site like a wagon train. He also discovered what the turn-of-the-century California architect Irving Gill realized many years ago: a traditional building of white masonry walls, once stripped of its decoration, quickly becomes modern. As a sculptor, Graham pushed the purity of the forms, sculpting the sphere, cylinder, and vault that Huston wanted, so that the California sun casts them in light, shade, and abstraction.

Several rooms adjoining the courtyard blur the boundary between inside and out. Wide, deep ledges at the kitchen windows invite food into the patio and guests into the kitchen. A row of French doors opens to a vaulted living room bookended by two outdoor walls of pure color

"I designed the forms and spaces exclusively for her," says Graham of his wife. "I followed her program. My responsibility to my client was met in having made her happy." LEFT: Two recycled-pinewood stairs descend from the bedroom: one leads to the bedroom, the other curves down to a bath. Project manager John Cordic executed the design.

"I don't know how to live sparely," says Huston, "but Bob does. With me, objects are apt to amass." Comments Graham, "I make things; I don't need to collect them." TOP: Billy Al Bengston's 1976 *Bahia Almejas Draculas* dominates Huston's second-floor study. Among the memorabilia is, at far left, her Oscar for Best Supporting Actress for *Prizzi's Honor* (1985).

"My collections started pre-birth," Huston says. ABOVE: The basement game room—its walls a counterpoint to the white stucco—is lined with artworks (by Jasper Johns, John Huston, and others) and photographs (including ones by Helmut Newton and Diane Arbus). "My objects follow me wherever I go. They remind me of who I am and where I came from."

brilliantly frescoed by New York artist David Novros: the intense Los Angeles sun seems to vaporize the yellow green and dark sepia, which shimmer in the light.

The studio next door in which Graham lived and worked for years once belonged to Doug Wheeler, a pioneer in California's light and space art movement. Wheeler experimented with apertures and baffles to sculpt light, and Graham learned the effects of the manipulations, bringing those notions to the design of his house. Some of the openings are shaped so that they feather incoming light across their natural plaster surfaces; others are tapered at their edges so that they appear to have no thickness, abstracting portions of the sky.

It was into this context of Graham's artistic concerns that Huston moved her furniture, not rushing in but fearing to tread. "I felt like a writer confronted by this beautiful vellum notebook that you then have to occupy," she says. "This is the first house of my own with a strong character, but I grew up in a strong house, so I know proper respect for them. The first night sitting in the living room reminded me of our drawing room in Ireland, at St. Clerans, which was grand rather than big.

"I'm used to decorating," she continues. "It's that old '60s gypsy thing when I modeled and had to make a place my own for four days—you know, scarves draped over shades, rat packing. I do it on location in my trailer, and I feel good—it's got to smell like me first."

Huston furnished her new house with objects that amount to a personal diary, and the ensemble turns the architecture into a home. "They're very real and important things from her mother and her father that she's lived with for years," says Graham. "She didn't just go out shopping."

The actor walks through the house, introducing pieces as though they were members of the family. "My father salvaged this tapestry of a harlequin from a

restaurant that was closing in Paris and hung it in his room in Ireland," she says. "These inlaid Moroccan chests were Mother's." The gold halo of a Greek Orthodox icon glimmers near a statuette centered on a desk: "The Oscar is mine." In the bedroom, a carved angel given to her at birth by a family friend hovers above the bed. A painting by Morris Graves is an abstraction of her mother, the ballerina Enrica Soma, who died in a car accident when Anjelica was a teenager.

If the furniture is a diary, the family album hangs in the billiards room, an engaging space perfumed by an adjacent cedar closet. Drawings of Huston by her father are displayed near pictures of father and daughter at all ages. A black-and-white photograph depicts Soma *en pointe* on a New York rooftop with her own mother and father, an Italian restaurateur. A portrait of Soma alone, wearing three strands of graduated pearls and smiling like the Mona Lisa, once graced the cover of *LIFE* magazine. The picture hangs next to an energetic Jasper Johns number painting, surrounded by more photographs by Robert Mapplethorpe, Herb Ritts, Helmut Newton, and Annie Leibovitz.

"Until the last two weeks, everything was covered with plywood," Huston says. "We were going on blind faith that the cumulative effort and all the decisions would work. And it was raining constantly. When we took the bandages off, it finally all made sense."

The house Graham designed for Huston may be 5,500 square feet, but it is a house that he has reduced to limpid simplicity. Bob on the bedroom balcony and Anjelica on the balcony of her study can speak across the coral tree to one another, and their voices carry in the quiet as a fountain murmurs below. Anjelica came off the hill into a house that wraps intimately around their relationship.

"With the courtyard and terraces, the house offers me a full interior and exterior life," Huston remarks. "I'm a Cancer. I have both of what I need here, which is comfort and places to escape to in the house and—so important—the sense of never feeling

ABOVE: The courtyard wall of the cantina-like kitchen is a David Novros fresco. Atop the kitchen is an open landing, which lies off Huston's study.

hemmed in." OPPOSITE: A lap pool forms the western edge of the courtyard. "It isn't finished," Graham says of the house. "We built into it its constantly changing nature: it will continue to be elaborated and worked on."

John Huston

Mercurial Director of *The Maltese Falcon* and *The Dead* at St. Clerans

TEXT BY LAWRENCE GROBEL
PHOTOGRAPHY BY LOOMIS DEAN

In 1952 John Huston had just begun making *Moulin Rouge*, which after its release would give him enough money to live anywhere in the world. Huston chose Ireland. He wanted a place to put everything he'd collected on his travels, and while staying at Courtown, he and his wife, Ricki, found the ideal spot in the western part of the country near Galway: a 110-acre estate called St. Clerans, whose three-story, seventeen-room house was in need of repair.

Huston went to see it, imagined what the manor would be like after workers spent a few years restoring it to its Georgian splendor, and told Ricki to buy it from the Land Commission for 10,000 pounds. Even though their marriage—her first, Huston's fourth—was sliding, the renovation of St. Clerans kept them together another seven years, before Ricki finally decided to move to London with the children.

St. Clerans provided Huston with a tranquil haven from his fervid pace of filmmaking, a place where he could paint, tend his horses, and entertain. Since dazzling Hollywood with his first picture, *The Maltese Falcon*, in 1941, Huston was in demand. He won two Oscars for writing and directing the 1948 film *The Treasure of the Sierra Madre*. Then came *Key Largo* (1948), *We Were Strangers* (1949), *The Asphalt Jungle* (1950), and *The Red Badge of Courage* (1951). But when *Red Badge* was taken away from him and edited down from more than two hours to sixty-one minutes, Huston got fed up and left the country to make *The African Queen* (1952). He wouldn't return to America to make another film for ten years.

During the nineteen years Huston owned St. Clerans, he made an average of one film a year. And of those films, only four were fully or partially made on Irish soil—*The List of Adrian Messenger* (1963), *Casino Royale* (1967), *Sinful Davey* (1969), *The Mackintosh Man* (1973). Which meant that for much of each year Huston traveled around the world, making such films as *Moby Dick* (1956), *Heaven Knows, Mr. Allison* (1957), *The Barbarian and the Geisha* (1958), *The Roots of Heaven* (1958), *The Unforgiven* (1960), *The Misfits* (1960), *Freud* (1962), *The Night of the*

Writer-director-actor John Huston, who won two Academy Awards for *The Treasure of the Sierra Madre* (1948) and was nominated twelve times for such films as *The Maltese Falcon* (1941), *The African Queen* (1952), and *Prizzi's Honor* (1985), lived at St. Clerans, his estate in west-ern Ireland, from the late 1950s to the 1970s.
ABOVE: In his basement office, Huston's Academy Award statuettes flank a Donatello award from Italy.
OPPOSITE: "The house itself was one of the most beautiful in all Ireland," wrote Huston about the Georgian residence in his autobio-graphy. The estate was an ideal place for him to indulge his passions—riding, painting, and entertaining.

TOP: "I like to mix good art," wrote Huston, describing the eclectic works in the main drawing room. "The fact that pieces are not of the same period and culture doesn't mean that they will not go together." At right is one of Monet's *Water Lily* paintings, and in the foreground is a Greek marble horse head.

ABOVE: In one hall, a deep red that Huston was fond of sets off Mexican mermaid sculptures on both sides of a tree-form candelabrum.

Iguana (1964), *The Bible* (1966), *A Walk with Love and Death* (1969), and *The Kremlin Letter* (1970). Ricki and the children, Anjelica and Tony, were left to enjoy the splendid isolation.

It was there that the children watched their father's films from 16-millimeter prints, put on dog and pony shows, played in the ruins of the Norman castle on the property, and fought imaginary battles with the IRA. For Anjelica, St. Clerans was a place to dress up in the costumes kept in a huge trunk. For Tony, it was a journey back in time. He studied falconry, fished in the estate's trout-filled stream, and traded his father's expensive gifts for the local kids' pop guns and toys.

Because of the drift in the Hustons' relationship, Ricki and the children lived in what was called the Little House, a comfortable three-bedroom house a half mile from the Big House, where Huston resided.

Ricki, who had a knack for such things, made Huston's house a home; Huston himself made it a museum where he stored and exhibited the art and artifacts he loved to collect: paintings by Miró, Gris, and Monet, a set of Toulouse-Lautrec posters, giant wooden crucifixes, pre-Columbian figures from Veracruz, and racks of practical and rare guns, along with the heads of a tiger and a water buffalo that he had shot on Indian and African safaris.

Journalist Alexander Walker, upon visiting St. Clerans, marveled at the art on the walls, the black-marble hallway, the silk screens from Japan, the Spanish Colonial chairs, the Napoleon bed, and the Inca and Aztec handiwork. "The effect was of a well-ordered treasure house into which the living Pharaoh would ultimately retire himself," he said.

Eloise Hardt MacNamara, a close friend and frequent visitor, recalled that there seemed to be so much scheming going on that the house could have been something out of de Sade. "Everybody had their little episode at St. Clerans," she said. "[Huston] had to forever have some intrigue and romance going on. The more intriguing and involved and black Irish it got, the better he liked it." A childhood friend of Anjelica's, Lizzie Spender, described Huston as "an old-fashioned king or sultan" and remembered people going in and out of different bedrooms late at night.

When he was in preproduction for his films, Huston often used St. Clerans to entertain writers, actors, and producers. Arthur Miller came to discuss *The Misfits*, Jean-Paul Sartre *Freud*, Marlon Brando *Reflections in a Golden Eye* (1967), and producer Ray Stark *The Night of the Iguana*, *Reflections*, and *Fat City* (1972). Once, Montgomery Clift came to stay to discuss his role as Sigmund

ABOVE: Huston enjoyed painting in his studio. "St. Clerans was a wonderful haven," he wrote. "When I came back from a trip abroad and entered that atmosphere, it was a world apart." RIGHT: Huston's portrait of his daughter, Anjelica. She and her brother, Tony, spent many of their childhood years at the estate, which was located near the seaside town of Galway.

Freud. When Huston saw a male reporter, who had come to interview Clift, emerging from Clift's room one morning, it was an indiscretion he couldn't forgive. "I don't care what he does," Huston would later say, "but I just didn't like having my nose rubbed in it." He took it out on the actor throughout the making of *Freud*, and in the end Clift would dub Huston a "laughing sadist."

John Steinbeck, also a frequent visitor, never thought of Huston that way. The writer was taken by the director's great charm. Huston even convinced the Nobel laureate to dress up as Santa Claus on Christmas Day. Steinbeck hoped to get even by writing about Daly, the ghost that Huston was convinced haunted St. Clerans, but he died before he was able to do so.

Everyone who visited Huston in Ireland seemed to come away with a different impression. To screenwriter Ben Maddow, he was a "Renaissance prince"; to Sartre, "a great Romantic, melancholic and lonely"; to novelist and *New Yorker* cartoonist William Hamilton, he, like Picasso, was a grand old man who liked to size himself up

LEFT: Huston luxuriates in his four-poster Florentine bed, carved and painted with doves and flowers. "I sometimes feel that I sold a little bit of my soul when I let St. Clerans go," he wrote.

RIGHT: "I had an entire Japanese bath, with shoji doors and mats, sent over and installed," wrote Huston. "The bath accommodated up to six bathers, and was wonderful for after hunting."

against other grand old men. "They're competitive sons of bitches, or they wouldn't be grand old men!"

Cici Huston, whom Huston made his fifth wife in 1972—when he was sixty-six and she thirty-two—found St. Clerans to be a strange and foreign place. "Cici was as out of place at St. Clerans as anyone could possibly be," Huston said. "This was a little half-Jewish princess from Hollywood in one of the oldest settings in Christendom." The new Mrs. Huston was shocked by the single women who came to visit and by how her husband mismanaged the staff and property. "After I saw the way things were run," she said, "I wanted to redo the books. I wanted to figure out where all the money was going." She also wanted to fire Huston's loyal staff—something he refused to do.

But within two years Huston put St. Clerans up for sale. His emphysema kept him from his beloved fox hunts, Cici had moved back to her house in California, and the cost of keeping the estate had quadrupled. Tony and Anjelica were saddened by the loss of their Irish home, but once Huston made the decision, he proceeded to rid himself of most of his possessions as well.

John Huston and Cici were divorced in 1975, and he went to live in primitive surroundings at Las Caletas, near Puerto Vallarta, Mexico, with his ex-wife's housemaid. He entered into his dark period of filmmaking, starting with *Wise Blood* (1979) and ending with *Under the Volcano* (1984), *Prizzi's Honor* (1985), and *The Dead* (1987). When he died on August 28, 1987, at the age of 81, his last words were, "Just give 'em hell!"

Danny Kaye

His Daughter Fondly Recalls Life at Home in Beverly Hills

TEXT BY DENA KAYE
PHOTOGRAPHY BY TIM STREET-PORTER

The house I grew up in still appears in that "Michelin to Movieland," the 2001 Souvenir Map and Guide to Starland Estates and Mansions. A few blocks north of Sunset in Beverly Hills, we were within earshot of Lucy and Desi, Pickfair, the Bennys, and Fred Astaire. As a little girl, I dreamed of living on a street with sidewalks like the ones I saw in *The Life of Riley*. I didn't have sidewalks, but my childhood did include the tinkling melody of the Good Humor Man, and the girl next door came over to ask if we could be friends. In those more relaxed years, we left the back door open and the car keys in the igni-

tion. There were no burglar alarms or gated entries with codes, so the milkman from Adohr Farms Dairy came in without knocking to deliver milk in glass bottles. Tour buses ventured up the long driveway, and some people actually caught my father on his way out the door.

My parents rented the house in 1949 and bought it a year later from the director Lewis Milestone, whose well-known films included *Mutiny on the Bounty* and *Of Mice and Men*. I finally sold it in 1992 after they had both died, and my life was elsewhere. But for more than four decades "the house," as we always called it, was an

BELOW: The wisteria-covered façade of the Kaye house in Beverly Hills.

anchor, a place where we could retreat and get grounded in our own way. My father, as he liked to say, would "flake out" on the couch for days at a time, watching talk shows, Julia Child and the Dodgers, and eating black licorice and BLTs. My parents preferred to entertain at home, and over the years they each developed their own style. It was also their place of business. My mother often sat at the piano in a corner of the living room 'til dawn, composing songs for my father's movies and stage appearances, like the Oscar-nominated *Five Pennies* (1959), and penning those wildly intelligent and fast-paced gems so associated with my father. We had the Airwick ready when Hollywood's cigar smokers came for meetings.

Above all, it was the home of a family that I always thought was not unlike many others in America, where we sometimes ate dinner in silence in front of the television and opened presents Christmas morning in pajamas. It was no big deal the night when, as a teenager, I answered the front door, dwarfed by an oversized bathrobe, my hair up in large rollers and Clearasil on every pore, to find myself facing Cary Grant. Ours was, I think, an ordinary, but at the same time a quite extraordinary, home.

The house was designed in 1932 for Mrs. R. B. Fudger by Roland E. Coate and soon after appeared in *Architectural Digest*. Our house has been characterized by

ABOVE: The George I oak sideboard in the bay window of the formal dining room displays several of the Kayes' Chinese export porcelain tureens and stands. The room was "usually used for big parties and sometimes for dessert after dinner in the Chinese kitchen," says Dena Kaye.

RIGHT: A candid moment at the piano with Danny, Dena, and Sylvia Kaye.

one architectural historian as "a stripped-down classical style best described as Regency." It was small by Hollywood standards, about 6,600 square feet, and perfectly proportioned. The siting of the house on the lot was unusual at the time. The motor court, set off by the purple hues of jacaranda trees and wisteria tumbling down the house's façade, sat at the end of the driveway and gave the property an estate feel in a suburban neighborhood.

The informal architects, however, were my parents, who each made contributions that changed how we lived. My mother was ahead of her time when she built a fifty-foot-long, eight-foot-wide, five-foot-deep, chlorine-free indoor lap pool and painted the enormous white satellite dish green to blend with the trees. She also created a media room when she winterized a solarium next to the living room. The music room (BLT spot) became the second heartbeat of the house, after the kitchen, and reflected how we lived. It was relaxed, warm, and invit-

ing, with cushy furniture in earth tones, a TV, hi-fi, bar, and black leather tables designed by my parents' good friend Fanny Brice. In our house, you didn't have to straighten out the cushions each time you got up.

The music room played a minor role in the swell dos my mother "produced" in the '50s. First of all, the invitations went out by Western Union. An Abbey Party Rents green-and-white-striped tent enclosed the back patio, outfitted with a dance floor, a bar, and ten tables of eight. These soirées were always black tie (she had a room full of Don Loper gowns), and place cards were de rigueur. The guest lists were vintage Hollywood. One party alone had the Humphrey Bogarts, George Cukor, the Ira Gershwins, the Kirk Douglases, and Groucho Marx. After dinner, people like Dinah Shore, George Burns, and Judy Garland sang, and my mother accompanied them on the piano. As for me, I'd hide on the landing of the staircase and watch everyone come in the front door.

Our lives changed considerably when my father started to cook. Black tie was out; in fact all ties were. It began innocently enough on Christmas mornings when he'd scramble eggs, onions, and green peppers and, over the years, progressed to tempura and linguine *al vongole*, all prepared on the old O'Keefe & Merritt in our cozy off-white kitchen. This room, with ruffled curtains and a huge island, was the pulse of our lives. My father, in particular, loved the tiny breakfast nook with walls full of cookbooks and an old-fashioned wooden table covered in a red-and-white-checked tablecloth. Many mornings he'd sit in his terry cloth robe, make phone calls, and offer a cup of coffee to whoever wandered in, like the plumber.

The seismic change came when he started an informal, self-appointed apprenticeship in Chinese cooking with the chefs at Johnny Kan's restaurant in San Francisco. This

OPPOSITE: Danny Kaye loved to cook and entertain in the Chinese kitchen, which he had equipped with several refrigerators, a stove with three woks, and an oven for cooking Peking duck.

ABOVE: The kitchen table is set for four, though Kaye preferred to serve eight, and never sat down until dessert.

ABOVE: "My mother had a separate building constructed for the fifty-foot-long, five-foot-deep indoor lap pool behind the house," Dena Kaye says. Beyond the glass doors at left are some of the orchids Sylvia Fine Kaye cultivated; to the right are the patio and the garden.

culminated in his buying a huge, stainless-steel Chinese restaurant stove, with three large woks, that required not only an extra gas line to the house but a whole separate room. And thus was born our Chinese kitchen, a twenty-five-by-twelve shedlike structure in the back alleyway where the laundry once hung and I used to roller-skate.

This auxiliary kitchen accommodated the stove, a vertical roasting oven, refrigerators, shelves reeling with strange-looking mushrooms and spices, and a round table that sat eight (his preferred number) with wood-framed chairs and black leather cushions. He found traditional lanterns in Chinatown and mixed them with modern ones from Copenhagen. No matter what he cooked—his delectable rack of lamb, key lime pie, feathery fettuccine made on his pasta machine, or omelettes for lunch—we ate in the Chinese kitchen. My mother called the "real" dining room "a vestigial remnant circa B.C., Before Chinese."

A nine-course Chinese meal was my father's tour de force. It took twenty-four hours of preparation under his total control. He checked his menu books (Sweet and Sour Cod, Chicken Hoi Sin, Tomato Flower Soup, Banjo

Duck) and guest lists so no one would eat the same thing twice. He shopped for everything himself at the Farmer's Market or Chinatown, and he chopped and pounded with his cleavers on a huge round butcher block in what he liked to call the "conventional kitchen," a glass door away from his Chinese culinary quarters.

People who came to our house for dinner learned the rules very quickly. If you were late, God help you. Informality reigned. Even the king of Sweden had to take off his tie. He drew from his many worlds, so an evening might include Zubin Mehta, Roddy McDowall, the Peter O'Malleys, and his bank teller. My father's Chinese kitchen was his private theater; he was the same entertainer at the stove as he was on stage. Audrey Hepburn said it was like watching a great ballet dancer. Rudolf Nureyev described him as "a balletic matador." Everyone got up to watch him cook (he never sat down until dessert), and once he'd carefully plated a dish and put it on the table, he'd bellow, like a drill sergeant, "Don't look at it! Eat it!" Would that I could still hear that command.

RIGHT: The master bedroom had French doors and a balcony overlooking the outdoor pool and the patio, where her parents often hosted dinner under a tent.

BELOW: In the entertainer's paneled study is a wall of memorabilia, including a gold record from the movie *Hans Christian Andersen* and a photograph of him conducting. Danny Kaye conducted orchestras around the world and raised millions of dollars for the Musicians Pension Fund.

Diane Keaton

The Actress's 1920s Bel-Air House Is a California Classic

ARCHITECTURAL AND INTERIOR DESIGN BY STEPHEN SHADLEY
TEXT BY NANCY COLLINS
PHOTOGRAPHY BY TIM STREET-PORTER

"When I was a little girl, my dad used to skin-dive off Palos Verdes, where there were these wonderfully warm and inviting Spanish Colonial houses," recalls Diane Keaton. "I remember being so taken by the graciousness of that indoor-outdoor living, the heat, the beautiful sun. Every aspect of that romantic myth of California appealed to me. As I got older, I further romanticized it . . . it lives on."

Indeed—and smack in the middle of Bel-Air no less. But then, Diane Keaton has always been a gal who likes creating things from scratch: characters, movies, books, houses—especially those she fell in love with during a California childhood memorable for trips to Hearst Castle and Mission San Juan Capistrano. "Those places were magical," she says. "Though, like everybody else, we lived in a Cliff May rip-off ranch house, my father was

always hunting out new homes, trying to invest in real estate. Some of my fondest memories are of going with him to open houses, looking at them, feeling the wonder of it all."

Three years ago Keaton focused that sense of wonder on an acre of land, reminiscent of those familial outings—"a very simple house with walls high enough that it felt like a mission. I loved its shape, how it sat on the property, that it was centered around a courtyard," or rather the "beginnings" of one, according to designer Stephen Shadley, whose thirty-year friendship with the actress has yielded collaboration on four of her homes. "I was so depressed when I first looked at that house," he laughs. "It'd been remodeled and refashioned so much, there was no sense of the vintage Spanish Colonial it once was. It had no magic of its own. I said, 'This is going

"It surprised me how long it took to find it," actress Diane Keaton says of her circa 1927 Spanish Colonial Revival house in Bel-Air, California (LEFT), lit by luminarias. Once settled on the structure, she asked her longtime friend and designer Stephen Shadley to restore it. OPPOSITE: The pair placed a Monterey club chair in the small sitting room off the stair hall.

ABOVE: A work by Charles Damrow hangs in the intimate dining room, sparsely furnished with a Monterey table and chairs and a Navajo rug. The ceiling beams are original; the ebonized-oak floors are new. Shadley designed the iron-and-mica chandelier.

RIGHT: Shadley fashioned a true-to-the-era arch leading from the kitchen and breakfast area to the dining room. The passageway is flanked by lighted display cases for pieces from the actress's extensive collection of colorful vintage Bauer and Catalina plates and pitchers.

OPPOSITE: "She's not afraid," Shadley says of Keaton, who is also a producer and a director. "She doesn't change things at whim, but if something isn't working, she's brave enough to say, 'Let's do another take.'"

to be a lot of work,'" which was fine by Keaton, who "liked the bareness of detail because I could change it. I don't get ideas right away—drawings mean nothing—only being in the space helps me redefine it. This wasn't a blank page. I have to work with something that exists, but there was a lot for me to do."

And the ever-game actress was up for it. "Diane prepared for this as for a film," says Shadley, "collecting photos, visual images, ideas in a loose-leaf binder, subdivided by room, that we constantly referred to."

Those references came in handy—especially when massive bedroom and kitchen restructuring required ceilings to be lifted, walls felled. Initially, the three upstairs bedrooms were meant to stay intact as "a separate place where I could be close to the kids, which is really important," she says, referring to eight-year-old daughter Dexter and four-year-old son Duke. "And since my bedroom wasn't the important room, I didn't care how big it was"—until it hit her that "as long as I'm doing such a big project, why not extend the upper story and add a balcony to create a master suite."

Equally complicated were the kitchen's four small, dark, oddball rooms now transformed into a spacious kitchen/family room combo featuring an enormous skylight as well as a fireplace with a mantel of dazzlingly colorful California tiles. "I'd always steered clear of color," she says, "because I don't know how to utilize it"—until, one day at a swap meet, eyeing the ubiquitous "California tile tables, going for $200 a pop, I thought, Wouldn't it be interesting to tear them apart and make a huge bar in the kitchen—which extended itself to the fireplace, cabana, and pool tiles. I bought up every tile in town," she says with a laugh.

The house's capacious living room meanwhile—even in its native state—offered its own special appeal. "The living room was always that room off to the left that was rarely used," she says, "whereas this was one you couldn't avoid." Adds Shadley: "Because you walk through it to get to the library and bedrooms, it was more passage than destination; it had a life. So we decided to treat it like a waiting room in a train station, with tiled wainscoting and iron-and-mica chandeliers"—the same light fixtures, in varying scales, used throughout. "Diane loves continuity, so you take a couple tricks and run with them, creating one big, moving space rather than different rooms with different personalities."

Equally consistent is Keaton's impressive array of Monterey furniture—the fruit of years of collecting pieces that spoke to her obsession with "the lifestyle that started in early-twentieth-century California. I take pride in being part of saving our history," she explains.

OPPOSITE: In the living room, *Canyon de Chelly*, a work by Edgar Payne, left, joins a 1937 oil by Pete Martinez, center, and Maynard Dixon's 1923 *The Grim Wall*. A hand-painted Monterey sofa and an art-tile table rest on a rug Shadley designed.

LEFT: Custom-made tile comprises the wainscoting and ledge—"good for showcasing paintings and antiques," says Shadley— throughout the living room. Among Keaton's beloved collections is one of cement "California" bears. The furnishings are Monterey; the rug is Navajo.

"California is a repository of startlingly unusual dwellings; every significant architect built a private home here, making the state a history of architecture in the twentieth century."

Her obsession with that lineage abounds: the beguiling Catalina and Bauer pots; the giant Hillside Pottery concrete vessels inlaid with California tiles; and, of course, the art—the sweeping desert and prairie landscapes of Maynard Dixon, Frank Tenney Johnson, Edgar Payne, Carl Oscar Borg. Even with the landscaping, she was unflinching in her mission, as it were, eschewing concrete in favor of the rough, golden beauty of decomposed granite, "like a dirt road but more reinforced— what you see walking into a mission. Everybody said, 'Don't do DG, it's sloppy. If women are in heels, they'll get dirty.' I said, 'No worry there; that's not me.'"

What *is* Diane Keaton, however, is this gloriously original version of her own Capistrano. "How do I feel living here? Secure," she muses. "I feel *safe*. Because the house is wrapped around a courtyard, there's a core that everything comes off of, making you feel somehow protected and walled in by the shape of the house. Everything looks inward, which is actually very soothing. It's like you're creating your own home," she pauses, "your own world."

ABOVE: An old factory table gains new life as a desk in Keaton's office, converted from what was once the garage. Photos, clippings, and ephemera—"Diane's visuals," says Shadley—fill a bulletin board in the room, which he created "as a private, separate work space for Diane."

LEFT: An adapted Robert Frost quote frames the kitchen, brightened by vintage California tile and a 1950s chrome O'Keefe & Merritt range. "We were driving around L.A. one day, and Diane saw the stove in a store window and said, 'Wait! Turn around and go back!'"

OPPOSITE: Keaton brought the master bedroom's Shadley-designed bed with her from her former residence in Beverly Hills. "We added a whole new structure to create a master suite with a balcony," says Shadley. The Calco sconces are 1920s.

BELOW: The California-tile-accented pool and cabana. Keaton, who shares her home with daughter Dexter, eight, and son Duke, four, says, "Frankly, what the children like best is the swimming pool. They spend a tremendous amount of time in the water, even in winter."

Jayne Mansfield

The Actress's Pink Palace on Sunset Boulevard

TEXT BY CHARLES CHAMPLIN
PHOTOGRAPHY BY ALLAN GRANT

Rudy Vallee bought the house in the 1930s but, for one reason or another, never lived in it. The style was what cynics have called Mediterranean Movie-Star Baroque, assertive but not quite achieving majesty. Not long after Jayne Mansfield and Mickey Hargitay were married in 1958, they began looking for a house that could become a proper symbol of their love and their rising celebrity. They were shown the house and found it ideal.

Mansfield had made a smash in *Will Success Spoil Rock Hunter?* on Broadway, playing more than 400 performances loosely wrapped in a towel as the "titular" head of a corporation in George Axelrod's satire on Hollywood, and she repeated the role in the 1957 movie (the target of the satire having been tactfully shifted to television). Hargitay, who had been Mr. Universe for a year, was one of an entourage of musclemen in Mae West's nightclub act at the Latin Quarter in New York—West billed him as "the most perfectly built man in the world." He and Mansfield met, and the electricity flowed.

The house at 10100 Sunset Boulevard sat on three and a half acres; it had (by their count) twenty-five rooms, including eleven baths. (City files say fifteen rooms, including seven baths.) By any count the price was right: $76,000, which even in those days was a considerable bargain. The owner, a grocery magnate, was eager to sell.

Mansfield and Hargitay retained Glenn Holse, who had designed Mansfield's Las Vegas nightclub act and was also the resident set designer for Steve Allen's television show, to decorate the house. Mansfield's favorite color had been pink ever since she was a little girl in Dallas. Accordingly, the house, previously unexceptional in white stucco, was repainted in a pink mixed with a generous salting of quartz grains that sparkled in the Southern California sun. A tall stone wall, also in pink, went up to surround the compound.

As befitted a many-chambered love nest, hearts and cupids became the prevailing motifs in the house, which soon became known as the Pink Palace. Hargitay, handy with his hands, built his wife a heart-shaped swimming pool. Across the bottom, in gold-leafed mosaic, he

"I believe in flashy entrances," said Jayne Mansfield, whose Pink Palace in Bel-Air epitomized the camp icon's screen and celebrity image in the early 1960s. RIGHT: Her collection of hundreds of magazine covers adorned the staircase—she appeared in *LIFE* as well as in *Playboy*. "Publicity has always come to me. I haven't gone to it," the actress once said. "But I've been cooperative."

spelled out in script, "I love you Jaynie." Her bath was floored, ceilinged, and walled in pink shag, and in the center was a heart-shaped tub with gold-leafed tiles and gold-plated fittings in the shapes of swans. The effect was of a cozy, furry pink cave.

The enormous living room was carpeted with deep white shag—her Chihuahuas had difficulty navigating it, and guests were asked to remove their shoes. The room featured cupid statues on pedestals in wall niches, a fountain equipped to circulate champagne, and a Steinway grand piano that, like the walls of the master bedroom, was painted with cupids.

"All my life," Mansfield once told a reporter, "I've dreamed of a place full of cupids and angels and hearts. It's too bad the drops of water from the fountain in the living room aren't heart shaped."

Ever since Shirley Temple had become her childhood idol, Jayne Mansfield dreamed of Hollywood stardom. Millions have shared the dream, but Mansfield went at it with relentless intensity. In 1954, when she was twenty-one, she persuaded her first husband, Paul Mansfield—whom she married at sixteen and who was just out of the army—to come to Hollywood with her and their baby, Jayne Marie. The aspiring actress began taking classes and making the rounds, often with the baby along in a stroller. Her husband found work as a roofer, but he grew to hate the town and the life and soon went back to Dallas.

Mansfield acquired an agent and inspired publicist named Jim Byron. He smuggled her on a press junket to a movie premiere in Florida, and, thanks to her endless posing at poolside in a minuscule bikini, Mansfield got more attention than the film or the stars. Together they built the Mansfield legend.

Her voluptuous figure, freely revealed, was central to her fame, of course, yet she possessed an oddly endearing mixture of innocence and calculation. She seemed alternately to be pushing sex and to be making fun of it, as Mae West did. She posed at the drop of a shutter, appearing at the openings of fried-chicken franchises and

"I would rather stay at home . . . and have a dinner before the fireplace," said Mansfield, who identified with her character in *The Girl Can't Help It*: "All she wants is to be a wife and mother, but sex keeps getting in the way."

LEFT: The lettering in the arabesque above the living room fireplace commemorated her marriage to Mickey Hargitay, who did much of the handiwork in the house. Her favored heart motif was quilted into the purple sofas.

ABOVE: The typewriter
carried the house's predomi-
nant color, pink, into the
red leather office.

charity events; she was Miss Freeway, Miss Electric Switch, Miss Fourth of July.

During her first year in California she finagled a screen test at Warner Bros. for *The Seven Year Itch* (1955), and, though she lost the part to Marilyn Monroe, Mansfield won a contract that led to roles in a dozen films over the next seven years. She appeared in Jack Webb's *Pete Kelly's Blues* (1955), *The Girl Can't Help It* (1956), and *Too Hot to Handle* (1960), and in 1968 a compilation of the sexiest sequences from her other films—*The Wild Wild World of Jayne Mansfield*—was released.

She grew famous with amazing speed, but all too quickly the dream began to fade. The good roles never materialized. She dreamed of being taken seriously as an actress. She was certainly a celebrity—"Celebrities don't *do*; they *are*," she once said proudly. But being a celebrity is not quite the same as being a star, and certainly not like being taken seriously as an actress.

With Hargitay, she had had three children: Miklos, or Mickey, Jr., born in 1958 while they were still living in a smaller house she had bought with an inheritance from her grandfather; Zoltan, born in 1960 in the new place;

ABOVE: The couple shared the Pink Palace with Powderpuff, a Pekingese, several Chihuahuas, and an ocelot. One of her *Playboy* spreads, partially shot in the pink bedroom, was banned in Chicago.

LEFT: Hargitay shaves in his own bathroom, with its black tile and gold-leaf mosaic counter. He did much of the work himself.

RIGHT: Mansfield traded promotional appearances for an estimated $150,000 worth of merchandise for the house, including the pink shag for the wall-to-wall, floor-to-ceiling treatment in the bath. She announced her ambition to have a house in Beverly Hills and a million dollars—and to be a star.

and Mariska, born in 1964. Although it was clear that Hargitay loved her desperately, she was drawn to others, especially those who told her they could help her career. In 1964 she divorced Hargitay and married Matt Cimber, who indeed managed her career and by whom she had a son, Anthony. But their marriage was tumultuous too, and divorce proceedings were in the works when Mansfield, three of her children, and her new lawyer-manager went to Biloxi, Mississippi, for a nightclub act during which she would sit on the laps of elderly gentlemen in the audience.

After the appearance, her car, traveling through heavy fog, slammed into and under a stalled semitrailer. The driver, Mansfield, and the lawyer-manager were killed instantly; the children—sleeping in the backseat—were injured but survived. Mansfield was only thirty-four.

The legal wrangling over her estate and the Pink Palace went on for years. Hargitay, who had remarried, raised the couple's children. Mansfield is buried in a family plot in Pen Argyl, Pennsylvania. The Pink Palace changed hands at least twice, and was demolished in November 2002.

OPPOSITE: She demanded "a heart-shaped house with a heart-shaped pool" as a precondition for her marriage to Hargitay. Though Mansfield bought it, she told reporters that the house, behind its iron gate with J and M entwined in a grillwork heart, had been a gift from her fiancé.

LEFT: Mansfield relaxes in the couple's forty-foot-wide pool surrounded by dozens of Jayne Mansfield Hot Water Bottles, a novelty item introduced in 1957.

Marilyn Monroe

The Nomadic Life of a Screen Legend

BY DONALD SPOTO

She was the most photographed woman in America, and very likely the most peripatetic. There was something of the pilgrim about her, for she was a ceaseless wanderer in search of herself.

The official certificate of her birth in Los Angeles on June 1, 1926, records her name as Norma Jeane Mortenson, but no one was quite certain of her father's identity. "I was probably a mistake," she said years later. "My mother didn't want me. I probably got in her way." This was an accurate assessment, for Gladys Baker, a nomadic flapper, gave her two-week-old baby over to the care of a foster family. For seven years the child lived with her grandmother's neighbors, Albert and Ida Bolender, a sober and devout couple, in a four-room bungalow in Hawthorne, near what is now Los Angeles International Airport.

"She didn't come very much," Monroe later said of her mother. "She was just the woman with the red hair."

But in 1933 Gladys swept out to Hawthorne, packed her daughter's meager wardrobe, and moved with her into a cramped apartment at 6012 Afton Place in Hollywood, near the studios where she worked as a film cutter alongside her equally bohemian friend, Grace McKee. Frequent trips to the movie palaces on Hollywood Boulevard—the Egyptian, the Chinese, the Pantages—now replaced Sunday school and hymn singing.

Within three months Gladys had obtained a bank loan, and in one afternoon moved everything she and her daughter owned into a six-room house at 6812 Arbol Drive, not far from the Hollywood Bowl. The item that settled Gladys's mind on this particular residence was a Franklin baby grand piano, painted white. For Gladys Baker, as for most Depression-era moviegoers, a white piano was a totem of better times.

Alas, they did not come, for Gladys, suffering from a violent reaction to some pills she'd taken for nervous tension, was carted off to a hospital psychiatric ward.

In 1935, after living with Grace McKee and then McKee's mother, Norma Jeane was moved to the Los Angeles Orphans Home. Her file described "a normal, healthy girl . . . who seems content and uncomplaining and also says she likes her classes." Even more, Norma Jeane liked the escape provided by the movies, and she was enchanted by McKee's suggestion that, with the right hair and makeup, she might be the next Jean Harlow.

During the next few years Norma Jeane was shuttled back and forth between the homes of friends and relatives. Fearing a return to the orphanage, in 1942, just weeks before her sixteenth birthday, she dropped out of high school to marry a handsome twenty-one-year-old named James Dougherty. "I never had a choice," she said.

Perhaps following a pattern set in her difficult childhood, Marilyn Monroe occupied a succession of residences throughout her life. OPPOSITE: In 1951, she furnished her Beverly Carlton Hotel apartment in Beverly Hills with books and a picture of Eleonora Duse—her most cherished belongings.

RIGHT: "I wish I had one-tenth of Marilyn's cleverness," said acting coach Natasha Lytess. "Whenever I arrived at her Doheny Drive apartment, she was studying."

"There's not too much to say about it. It was like a dream that never really happened. I guess we were too young."

Ensconced in a one-room bungalow in Sherman Oaks, she tried to rise to the demands of being a suitable housewife for an independent if kindly fellow who was soon to ship out to war, and from whom, after four years of mostly separate lives, she would be divorced.

When Dougherty was sent to the Southeast Asian war zones, Norma Jeane felt abandoned once again. A drab life with her mother-in-law in North Hollywood was relieved by work at the Radioplane Company in nearby Burbank—where she was first photographed by an army motion-picture unit in 1945. "An army corporal by the name of David Conover told me what to wear and what shade of lipstick, etc.," Norma Jeane wrote to Grace McKee, "and he said that by all means I should go into the modeling profession . . . that I photographed very well. He is *strictly* business, which is the way I like it."

By the spring of 1945 she was becoming known among Los Angeles photographers as a dream subject. Cooperative, eager, and full of good humor, she tossed her curly, chestnut-colored hair, flashed her blue-green eyes, smiled brightly, and gazed unblinkingly at the camera. Something fresh and lively seemed to spring to life just before the shutter clicked or the film rolled.

An appointment with a movie studio was perhaps inevitable, and a screen test at Fox in July 1946 led to her name change and a contract that paid her $75 a week. Only when it was renewed for a second six months was she finally cast in her first too-negligible roles (in *Scudda-Hoo! Scudda-Hay!* and *Dangerous Years*, both in 1948). But no one took much notice of just another pretty contract player.

In 1948 Monroe moved to the Studio Club in Hollywood, a two-minute walk from the Los Angeles Orphans Home. "I felt like I was living on my own for the first time," she would say. From there she went to Columbia Studios, at Sunset and Gower, where she sang in a B movie called *Ladies of the Chorus* (1948). There too she met her first drama coach, an intense woman named Natasha Lytess. By the summer of 1949 she had also met the powerful William Morris Agency executive Johnny Hyde. Thirty-one years her senior, he was instantly besotted, left his family, and moved with Monroe into a

ABOVE: After spending several months on the East Coast, Monroe returned to California in 1956 for *Bus Stop*. During filming she lived with photographer Milton Greene and his wife, Amy, in a house near UCLA.

rented house at 718 North Palm Drive, which she tried to enliven with reproductions of great art she had clipped from books—Fra Angelico, Dürer, and Botticelli were among her favorites. At her bedside she placed a framed photo of Eleonora Duse. "Johnny inspired me to read good books, to enjoy good music, and he started me talking again. I'd figured early in life that if I didn't talk I couldn't be blamed for anything."

But she still maintained a one-room cinder-block apartment at the modest Beverly Carlton Hotel on Olympic Boulevard, where she got mail. Thanks to Hyde, she also began to receive paychecks—for small roles in (among a half dozen pictures) *The Asphalt Jungle* and *All About Eve* (both 1950). Her screen time was brief, her impact tremendous.

In 1950, just before Hyde's death, Monroe accepted an offer from Natasha Lytess to share her apartment in West Hollywood. She brought with her some books, pictures, and records, and her wardrobe, which consisted of a few sweaters and skirts. This constituted her entire list of possessions until shortly before her death; she cared little for things, owned no jewelry, and vigorously denied

that diamonds could ever be a girl's best friend. "I'm not interested in money," she once told an agent. "I just want to be wonderful."

Life with her coach was appropriately simple: she slept on a living room daybed, helped care for Lytess's daughter, studied plays, demolished the apartment's neatness, and (ever conscious of her aborted education) dashed out for a ten-week evening course in world literature at UCLA.

Her first starring role, as a psychotic babysitter in *Don't Bother to Knock* (1952), was a remarkable achievement: in a performance of extraordinary density and subtlety, Marilyn portrayed not a stereotypical madwoman but the recognizable casualty of a wider urban madness. "I'm trying to find myself now, to be a good actress and a good person," she told a reporter outside the Beverly Carlton one morning. "Sometimes I feel strong inside, but I have to reach in and pull it up. It isn't easy. Nothing's easy. But you go on." And with that she leaped on her bicycle for the ten-minute ride to Fox.

In 1951 and 1952, swiftly attaining stardom, Monroe had nine films in release—and added no less than three

ABOVE: Eight months before her death Marilyn Monroe discovered a Spanish-style house in the Brentwood section of Los Angeles.

addresses to her biography. In her small one-bedroom at 882 North Doheny Drive, she began her romance with Joe DiMaggio in 1952. "Almost any place would have done for me," she told a friend, "but I tried to make it homey for Joe." To that end, she learned to cook spaghetti (which pleased him) and to decorate a room with framed, instead of taped, art reproductions (to which he was indifferent).

The marriage of two American icons, Monroe and DiMaggio, took place in January 1954, and for several months they rented a furnished mock-Tudor house at 508 North Palm Drive in Beverly Hills. Soon both the rooms and the marriage were in disarray, at least partly because her star was on the ascendancy and DiMaggio was in retirement. From the house she drove to the studio for *There's No Business Like Show Business* (1954) and *The Seven Year Itch* (1955), and on the front lawn in October 1954 she and her attorney announced the end of her marriage to DiMaggio after less than a year.

Unwilling to be treated capriciously by either a boss or a husband, Marilyn Monroe walked out on her studio contract in 1955 and lived in Weston, Connecticut, with photographer Milton Greene and his wife, Amy. For the next three years she and Greene were partners in Marilyn Monroe Productions. "I am tired of the same old sex roles," she told the press. "I want to do better things. People have scope, you know."

Also in 1955 she began attending classes at the Actors Studio in New York. For her Manhattan base, the fledgling production company took a six-month lease on a twenty-seventh-floor suite in the Waldorf Towers (whose other residents included Cole Porter, the Duke and Duchess of Windsor, and General MacArthur). The apartment's furnishings were almost all white, her favorite color scheme since she believed it was also Jean Harlow's. She invited the press—and Arthur Miller, whom she was dating regularly and whom she married in the summer of 1956.

Earlier that year she moved back to Los Angeles for interior studio work on *Bus Stop*. She and the Greenes rented a furnished house at 595 North Beverly Glen Boulevard in Bel-Air. When they left just three months later, the house was a shambles—the result of wild parties and an atmosphere in which there was a prodigious consumption of alcohol and drugs. "I want to live quietly in the country," Monroe told Arthur Miller after completing her brilliant performance as Cherie the "chantoosie" in *Bus Stop*.

She got her wish later that year in England, when after their marriage the Millers were installed at Parkside House for the shooting of *The Prince and the Showgirl* (1957). Situated on ten acres, the house had five bedrooms and quarters for servants. From this serene environment the actress traveled to the studio, where things were far less congenial. She and costar Laurence Olivier had different methods of preparation and performance; Marilyn Monroe Productions was badly organized and managed; and the marriage to Miller was already in jeopardy. Despite all this, she shone in a comic and poignant triumph.

Back in New York, the Millers rented an apartment at 444 East 57th Street and, with the help of designer John Moore, Monroe played interior decorator. She made one large room of two, creating a living/dining area; she mirrored several walls and had others painted stark white. But to Monroe, the apartment, like her performances, was never "right," and she was constantly remodeling, changing furniture, draperies, and accessories.

In 1958, having endured the collapse of her production company and the end of her relationship with the Greenes, three miscarriages and severe depressions in the aftermath of each, Monroe went back to work in Hollywood. The film, *Some Like It Hot* (1959), was her second with Billy Wilder, for whom the experience was exhausting. Her marriage was now in trouble, she was drinking far too much, and doctors were prescribing sedatives in dangerous amounts.

Monroe returned to East 57th Street in 1959 weary and worn out, but she worked with Miller on improvements to their house in Connecticut—the first one she had ever owned with anyone. There and in Manhattan, she invited such luminaries as Carson McCullers, Isak Dinesen, and Carl Sandburg for simple suppers. Empty hours depressed her, however, as her friend Susan Strasberg remembered, "and she was bored with the role of country housewife." In 1961, just before the premiere of *The Misfits*, her last film, she divorced Miller.

Returning to California, Monroe lived mostly in hotels. The rooms were merely a base from which she dashed out for visits to doctors and a psychiatrist, and for meetings with agents, publicists, writers, and producers.

Finally, a few months before her death, she found a home. In the Brentwood section of West Los Angeles, the actress fell in love with a Spanish-style hacienda at 12305 Fifth Helena Drive. Secluded and private, the 2,300-square-foot house needed refurbishing, but it had

a tile roof, thick white stucco walls, a beamed cathedral ceiling in the living room, and arched doorways throughout. The property also had lush plantings and a swimming pool—all nestled on a quiet cul-de-sac.

In early 1962 she planned a partial renovation of the house and went to Mexico to shop for furniture, cushions, and tapestries and looked for tiles to install in her new

ABOVE: Though she was waiting for the delivery of furniture, she brought along her books and records.

kitchen and baths. "Marilyn was very happy," recalled her friend Ralph Roberts. "She was really taking control of her life and asserting herself." All those close to her agreed.

Most of her purchases were still undelivered when she died, and so her dream of a place of her own was never fulfilled. But her desire to leave a legacy was—in twenty-nine films. She still stands for something funnily unsolemn about sex, something truthful and vulnerable.

Director Joshua Logan called Monroe "one of the great talents of our time—warm, witty, extremely bright, and totally involved in her work. Hollywood shamefully wasted her." To this day, that assessment is endorsed everywhere by millions. When Marilyn Monroe died on August 4, 1962, her life was not in decline but full of promise.

TOP: The living room features high-beamed ceilings and tilework. She traveled to Mexico in February 1962, enthusiastically searching shops in Cuernavaca, Taxco, Toluca, and Acapulco for fabrics, furniture, and tiles for her new home.

ABOVE: A woven textile hangs in the sun porch. In the dining room beyond is a chandelier in the shape of a star. "I've spent most of my life running away from myself," she said six years earlier. "But after all, I'm a mixture of simplicity and complexes."

OPPOSITE: Monroe in her last photo session, for *LIFE* magazine. She died a month later. "My home? It will be a place for any friends of mine who are in some kind of trouble. As for me, I just want to be an artist and an actress with integrity."

Dennis Quaid

A Serene Life for the Actor Amid the Rolling Hills of Montana

TEXT BY NANCY COLLINS
PHOTOGRAPHY BY DAVID O. MARLOW

"Montana is what I always wanted Texas to look like," says actor and Texas native Dennis Quaid. "Houston is very flat, and though I love the Hill Country of Austin, Montana is still what every boy from New York thinks Texas is."

In the 1970s, when this Texas boy went looking for the celluloid version of his roots, he landed in Montana's Paradise Valley, a sixty-mile stretch of land between Livingston and Yellowstone National Park. Though it's gone on to become, much to native dismay, a favorite getaway haven for the rich and famous, in those days it was only the truly hip who made their way to Big Sky—people like Quaid and actor Warren Oates.

OPPOSITE: Aspen and fir trees surround the wood-and-stone residence of actor Dennis Quaid, on five hundred acres once partly owned by actor Warren Oates in Montana's Paradise Valley. At right is the observatory. "I was into astronomy as a kid," says Quaid. "Now I sit and watch the stars."

LEFT: Quaid and his chocolate Labrador retriever, Henry, beside a turn-of-the-last-century cabin along a pond he put in near the main house. The cabin has an adjacent dock from which the actor fly-fishes. The property, which he named Camp Warren Oates, is used year-round.

"When I was building on my original property, I lived with Warren," recalls Quaid of his original 160 acres, "and after he died, I bought the house from his widow." Later, when another Montana "pioneer," director Sam Peckinpah, passed on, Quaid picked up further acreage "three miles down the valley"—a hop, skip, and a trot in Montana terms. Finally, five hundred acres down, Quaid, in a nod to his old buddy, dubbed his place Camp Warren Oates and started thinking about building his own "dream house." In 2000 he finally did—coming up with a 7,800-square-foot, three-bedroom rock-and-log ranch house so indigenous in feel it might well have been on the prairie when buffalo, not Range Rovers, roamed.

For most of its yearlong construction Quaid was able to be on-site—a process he found remarkably similar to that of another passion: filmmaking. "I've directed a movie, and it's a lot like building a house," says the actor. "You're called upon to have opinions on everything. On a movie set and a construction site, everyone is always asking what you think. I never thought of myself as a detail person, but I found out that I very much am—that, in fact, I have something to say about everything. Your opinion, after all, is what dictates your taste—good or bad."

In Quaid's case, the good—and the old—won out. "I wanted a house that looked old," says Quaid, "as if it had been built in stages over a long period of time." He also says he wanted space—lots of it. "I do not," he says emphatically, "like dinky."

OPPOSITE: Quaid found the great room's black leather sofa and chairs in Austin, Texas, where he shopped for many of the house's furnishings. "I just grabbed the pottery from different places," he explains. The fireplace is made from Montana stone. The doors lead to a sleeping porch.

ABOVE RIGHT: The great room holds Quaid's guitars and piano. An avid musician, the actor has written songs for several of his films and serves as the front man for his band, Dennis Quaid and the Sharks. Austin-based designer Donna Stockton-Hicks helped him select and place the furniture. BELOW RIGHT: The wraparound porch. The architect, Montanan Frank Cikan, says the 7,800-square-foot structure "began as a cabin that just kept growing and growing."

"I wanted muted colors," says Quaid. "And I wanted the house to look as if it had been here, in the wild, for one hundred years." LEFT: The oak table and benches in the dining room came from director and screenwriter Sam Peckinpah, who lived in a cabin on nearby land purchased by Quaid.

To articulate his grand vision, Quaid called upon Montana architect Frank Cikan, who admits that the original plan was to build a simple cabin for guests—until, that is, Quaid decided to make a home for himself. "Suddenly, we went from a 2,600-square-foot cabin to a 7,800-square-foot house," says Cikan. "So I came up with the concept of one main house with two additions, as if it had evolved over time."

Beyond that, Quaid was determined to turn the spectacular natural landscape into a design device. "In Montana, you spend a lot of time outdoors, and I wanted to bring that in—with large windows and lots of doors. I once saw a monastery in Greece that had one hundred doors. We don't have that many, but we have a lot."

When it came to the exterior, Quaid was equally decisive. "Coming from Texas, I loved the rock houses there," he says, a notion he coupled with logs for the authentic Montana feel. But instead of the logs "having really straight lines," he wanted the rough edges of weathered-looking wood. "At first the guys were aghast when I said, 'Go ahead and put a big cut in them. Take

OPPOSITE: Centering the kitchen, which is accessible from the dining room through a stone walkway, is a two-sided fireplace that adjoins the great room. Throughout the house, distressed and stained planks salvaged from the Great Chicago Fire of 1871 are used as flooring.

RIGHT: A guest room's bed was crafted by the architect and bears the Camp Warren Oates logo—a crescent moon, a mountain, and a rising sun. Quaid asked for the red leather to be added to the headboard. The bedside table is Arts and Crafts style; the rug is an antique Sarkoy kilim. BELOW: The master suite overlooks a stand of trees behind the house. Above the bed, which Quaid purchased from actress Sandra Bullock, is a photograph of the cast of Buffalo Bill's Wild West show. A nineteenth-century Ersari rug is on the floor.

out a piece, scrape it. I don't care if it looks even, because in the end it will add up to a whole.'"

In terms of the interior, Quaid took on the job himself, with the help of friends like director and screenwriter Callie Khouri, who picked out the oversize black leather sofa and chairs in the great room, a massive thirty-by-sixty-foot space, built around a magnificently imposing, four-by-five-foot fireplace surrounded by Chief Joseph stone whose mantel and hearth each consist of a sixteen-foot-long slab of stone.

Perhaps the most beautiful piece of furniture in the house—a spectacular oak picnic table seating ten—came courtesy of Sam Peckinpah. "It was in Sam's cabin. In fact, I think he built it," says Quaid. "It's all pegged, not a single nail in it, just a beautiful piece. It ends up being the dining room table, because we're real casual around here." As a matter of fact, the cook usually ends up being the owner himself. "I do most of my own cooking

up here," says Quaid. "From my other house I learned how to situate the kitchen so all you have to do is turn this way and reach the stove, that way and get to the sink. The fireplace in the kitchen?" He chuckles. "That's an Irish idea."

What Quaid was after for his interiors, he says, was "a Craftsman feel, with lots of Arts and Crafts, but with an Eastern influence—Buddhas and Shivas all around. I've always been taken with the simplicity of Eastern architecture. I think that Arts and Crafts style is really derived from Eastern lines."

That mélange of West/East sensibilities is exquisitely exemplified in the master suite, with its romantic, 180-degree views that encompass the Gallatin Range, Emigrant Peak, and one of the property's man-made ponds. As you enter the spacious bedroom, your eye immediately goes to the image hanging over the bed— "a rare photograph of Buffalo Bill's Wild West show," explains Quaid, "rare because everybody had to stand still for twenty minutes." The bed itself, stunning black-painted wood, is purposefully draped in "Buddhist colors of bright orange and red."

BELOW: He chose a trough sink for his bath.

OPPOSITE: One of two ponds on the property reflects Quaid's annual Fourth of July fireworks and the surrounding mountainscape. "I'm so pleased with the way the house is settling in here, even though the deer keep eating my aspens," says Quaid. "It gets more beautiful to me all the time."

RIGHT: Quaid with Henry and Clyde, who catches a ride on Jupiter Ray, one of five horses roaming the camp. "I keep them well away from the house—so we can't smell them," he quips. "My next project is to build them a big barn of their own."

BELOW: Henry, June, and Slim rest on the steps of the bluestone-paved porch. At right is the sleeping porch, requested specially by Quaid for the house. The actor, whose handicap is two, drives golf balls from the lawn fronting the residence. The Gallatin Range is in the distance.

"The bed actually belonged to Sandra Bullock," confesses Quaid, who caught an ad Bullock had placed in Austin's *Recycler*. "Sandra was moving to another house in Austin, and when she wound up staying where she was, the bed she'd bought for the new house didn't fit. So I called and said, 'I saw your ad in the *Recycler*.'" Sandra, he wryly notes, did not come with the bed.

Though besotted with the chairs, pictures, and architectural style of Arts and Crafts, Quaid admits he has his limits. "I don't like their couches," he says, "because they're like library couches—not comfortable."

With that in mind, in the bedroom, he opted for a mammoth Roycroft chair, over which hangs, not surprisingly, a rendering of a Buddha—not indicative, he hastens to add, of a particular philosophical predilection. "I meditate and have been to India six times, but no, I'm not anything. Let's put it this way, I believe in it all."

If anything made Quaid a believer in the talent and skill of Montana artisans, it was simply watching them ply their craft. "It was a great experience working with the craftsmen, watching the thing slowly take shape"— a great, if expensive, experience. "You spend more money," he laughs, "because when you're there, you keep changing things."

Like the time Quaid decided to reconfigure the wraparound Pennsylvania bluestone porch. "They were in the middle of doing the porch, and I had them stop and repour the foundation, because it was too small." Apparently, it paid off. "I love its lines," he says, "the way it juts out with its rustic Arts and Crafts fixtures." Its veranda-like feel, meanwhile, is a clear throwback to Quaid's "southern upbringing. Did I have a porch growing up in Texas? No, but I always wanted one."

He also wanted to live with very specific colors. The golden sheen of the great room, for instance, mimics "the way the Montana grass looks in late summer and fall. I wanted that brought inside," along with, he adds, the muted greens covering the walls in the rest of the rooms.

As serene and peaceful as the house is, it is not without whimsy. Hanging out in the sleeping porch, a giant stuffed bear holds court. "It's a good thing to put outside people's rooms on their first night here," laughs Quaid. Other special features came from his son, Jack, who requested bunk beds and got them—custom-made queen-size bunk beds—along with a tree house.

"It's boy heaven up in here," says Quaid. "In fact, Montana should just drop the *o* for *a*—'Mantana.' They have so much space to run around in, all the wildlife, the fishing, the go-carts. Like I said, kid heaven."

Not to mention providing a celestial moment or two for Dad, an astronomy buff who has a sixteen-inch reflector telescope in his observatory on the property. "When I'm in Montana, my mind is able to expand out over the entire valley," muses Quaid. "With my life often being so social, it's nice to be up here in the peace and quiet, to commune with myself." He pauses, chuckling. "And, man, I can go out my front door, turn left, and go one hundred miles without crossing a road."

Ronald Reagan

Revisiting the Actor and Former President's Domestic Policies

TEXT BY JOHN MERONEY

Ronald Reagan has always been enchanted by views. As a Hollywood star, he would walk dinner guests out by his swimming pool in Pacific Palisades and show them the sweeping vista of Los Angeles at night. When he moved to Washington, D.C., Reagan would take visitors to the family quarters of the White House, look out across the Ellipse and, under the white dome by the Tidal Basin, introduce them to one of his heroes. "Thomas Jefferson," he would say, pausing for dramatic effect. "I look at him from here, and he looks at me."

Reagan's first view of Los Angeles was in 1937. He had left his job as a radio announcer at WHO in Des Moines to take a two-hundred-dollar-a-week job at Warner Bros., traveling by car at breakneck speed to get there. "I got a cramp in my foot and somehow or other couldn't get it off the gas pedal," he said in an interview after arriving. Cruising into town, the top down on his Nash convertible, he could smell the scent of orange blossoms in the air.

In 1940 Reagan beat out John Wayne, William Holden, and Robert Young for the movie part he loved more than any other: Notre Dame football star George Gipp in *Knute Rockne—All American*. In 1981 President Ronald Reagan would tell Notre Dame students that the film used the "uniquely American" sport of football to tell a story about sacrifice, commitment, and morality. Rockne, he said, was symbolic of American virtues.

"California isn't a place," Reagan once observed. "It's a way of life." And the kind of life he was living there often seemed charmed. By New Year's Eve 1940, he was looking back at the last twelve months with a true sense of accomplishment. Jack Warner was calling the young actor his number-one star, ranking him ahead of James Cagney and Humphrey Bogart; the studio had raised his weekly salary to almost two thousand dollars; and MCA executive Lew Wasserman was guiding his career. And almost a year earlier he had married actress Jane Wyman, whom he had met on the set of *Brother Rat* (1938).

The newlyweds were living in a two-bedroom apartment on Londonderry View, above what is today the Sunset Plaza section of West Hollywood. The Art Mod-

Reagan married Nancy Davis in 1952; in 1957 the couple moved into their hillside house in Pacific Palisades. BELOW: The living room.

erne building had rounded walls and Art Deco tile work. Adding to its allure was a magnificent view of the city.

"All of Dad's places were selected with that in mind," his daughter Maureen said of her father's affinity for views. One room of the apartment was Reagan's office. His desk was a replica of George Washington's, a gift from Wyman after she had noticed Reagan's fascination with the real one during a tour of Mount Vernon in 1940.

In the 1940s Reagan was making films such as *Santa Fe Trail*, starring with Errol Flynn, Raymond Massey, and Olivia de Havilland. In *Kings Row*, he was a man about town who meets with disaster in a train wreck and later wakes up to discover that doctors have amputated his legs. He cries out in terror, "Where's the rest of me?"—a line that he later used as the title of his autobiography. During World War II Reagan was a captain in the army, but because severe myopia prevented him from serving in combat, he helped administer the Army Air Forces First Motion Picture Unit, which made military training films.

Mostly, however, the real drama in Ronald Reagan's life was taking place offscreen. He had become an active board member of the Screen Actors Guild in 1941, and in 1947 he was elected president, placing him at the center of the controversy about Communist Party activity in the entertainment industry.

Although Reagan willingly testified before the House Un-American Activities Committee, he resented government interference in his company town and admitted that the HUAC crowd was a "pretty venal bunch." But it

Before entering politics, Ronald Reagan (LEFT) lived the quintessential Hollywood life as a film star and television host.

The Reagans lived in the house until moving to Washington, D.C., in 1981. TOP: Movies were screened in the dining room via a hidden projector.

ABOVE: Sliding glass doors in the den offered a view to the Pacific Ocean.

BELOW: During his Illinois youth Reagan had been a lifeguard, and he remained an avid swimmer well into adulthood.

BOTTOM: The Reagans' house typified the California contemporary style of architecture that reached its pinnacle in the 1950s.

was firsthand experience with defiant Communists in the labor strikes and their threats of physical violence against him that was the catalyst for his change from a New Deal liberal to a Republican conservative.

On a more personal level, his marriage was crumbling. In 1941 Reagan and his wife had built an eight-room house on Cordell Drive above Sunset, where they were raising Maureen and, later, their adopted son, Michael. But Reagan's increased involvement with the Screen Actors Guild, his burgeoning passion for politics, and the realization that things with Wyman weren't meant to be all culminated in a 1948 divorce.

In the late 1940s and early 1950s Reagan was starring with Patricia Neal in *John Loves Mary* and *The Hasty Heart*, Virginia Mayo in *The Girl from Jones Beach*, and Doris Day in *Storm Warning*. He was also back in the Londonderry View apartment: rich, handsome, driving around town in a Cadillac convertible, spending seven hundred and fifty dollars a month on nightclubs and dating some of his costars. "Obviously this pattern of living was acceptable if you didn't look more than forty-eight hours ahead," Reagan wrote.

Then, as he told biographer Edmund Morris, "along came Nancy Davis and saved my soul." Over dinner with the MGM actress at LaRue's on Sunset in 1949, he calmed Davis's fears that she might be blacklisted because someone with a similar name was suspected of involvement in Communist-front groups. He was also falling in love.

But as Reagan himself has confessed, "This story, I know, will be a disappointment to those who want romance neatly packaged. The truth is, I did everything wrong, dating her off and on, continuing to volunteer for every Guild trip to New York—in short, doing everything which could have lost her if Someone up there hadn't been looking after me." True love finally won out, and Ronald Reagan, forty-one, and Nancy Davis, twenty-eight, were married in 1952.

With the quality of film scripts being offered to him in decline, Reagan turned to television in 1954, signing on as host of *General Electric Theater*, a weekly CBS anthology series. With him aboard, the program generated larger audiences than Arthur Godfrey, Red Skelton, Perry Como, Jack Benny, and even *Gunsmoke*. General Electric also began using Reagan as a corporate spokesman, touring the country with a message about how government regulation was stifling the free enterprise system. His speeches resonated, and the company rewarded Reagan handsomely.

In 1955 General Electric helped him begin building a modern ranch-style house on San Onofre Drive, in Pacific Palisades, that he designed with architect William

Stephenson. "The whole area really wasn't developed then," says son Ron Reagan, born in 1958. "I remember there was this dirt road that went up into the hills, and we'd go up there and fly kites. Now I think there's a castle there."

Nancy Reagan says that one of the objectives was to accentuate the view. As one walks through the 5,000-square-foot house, the city and the Pacific Ocean are visible from all the main rooms. And when it came to cutting-edge accoutrements, G.E.'s technicians went all out. "I can't tell you how many refrigerators, ovens, and fancy lights G.E. gave us," Nancy Reagan recalls. "They even put in a garbage disposal, which was unique for the time."

The house included a dining room that was custom-made for a movie star. Hidden behind a painting that would slide to one side was a projector. "That actually got put to a lot of use," says Ron Reagan, who remembers screenings of home movies and studio films.

Out by the octagonal swimming pool was an extensive lighting system. "Because there were so many wires and switches, we built a special panel on the side of the house," says Nancy Reagan. "Whenever we had people over for dinner, Ronnie would tell them we had a direct link to the Hoover Dam." (Such a link would have been of great help when the house was almost destroyed by a brush fire in 1977. "I remember helping my parents evacuate," says Ron Reagan. "We were throwing the silverware in the pool.")

One of the most memorable occasions had to be the evening of November 4, 1980—the night Reagan got the part that became, as biographer Lou Cannon calls it, the role of a lifetime. "I'll never forget that night," says Nancy Reagan. "It was just after five, so it was already nighttime on the East Coast. I took a bath, and Ronnie got in the shower. In the background I could hear John Chancellor on the TV in the bedroom, and suddenly he says Ronnie's won—in a landslide. So I jumped out of the tub, started banging on the shower door, and we ran to the TV. There we were, standing in our towels, listening to them say he had been elected. Then the phone started ringing. It was President Carter, calling from Washington to concede the election and to congratulate Ronnie on winning."

When asked about the common thread of the dramatic views that runs through all his father's Hollywood homes, Ron Reagan pauses. "You know, some people like to live in valleys," he says. "My dad just always loved mountains."

TOP: The Reagans (including Ron, in high chair) at breakfast, circa 1959. General Electric filled the kitchen with new appliances.

ABOVE: The slate-floored entryway included a guest closet and a powder room which connected to a pool-area shower and dressing room.

Martin Scorsese

An 1860s Town House for the *Age of Innocence* Director

TEXT BY JUDITH THURMAN
PHOTOGRAPHY BY DURSTON SAYLOR

Edith Wharton invented the semiotics of real estate. She could parse a block of New York like a sentence and tell you what the location of each house signified. The moves of her characters—the brownstones or mansions that they buy, sell, build, lose, or inherit—help define them.

Martin Scorsese's New York—the Little Italy of his childhood and his early films—was as much of a circumscribed, defining province as Wharton's. As a boy he observed its boundaries: he never even ventured as far north as Greenwich Village. As a man and an artist, he has reckoned with its pull. "I'm a die-hard New Yorker, but I've spent my life making movies and living on location. When I was ready to make a home for myself, I didn't know what style of living in Manhattan would make me feel most comfortable. It depends where you

start from. I started from the Lower East Side tenements. I certainly wasn't going back to Elizabeth Street. But where did I belong?"

Scorsese settled that question definitively in the early 1990s, when he moved to an Upper East Side town house with a walled garden—not so grand as the mansions of *The Age of Innocence*, but built in the same period. The neighborhood, he says, "has a small-town feel to it, even with a busy avenue on the corner." And in the small hours of the morning, when the traffic has subsided, he can sometimes hear the sound of a horse and carriage passing under his windows. It helps him imagine, he says, what Wharton's New York felt like.

The town house has also given the director "a sense of permanence" that had been elusive. "I've tried high-rise

"There's a part of me that loves a kind of Japanese minimalism—I need an uncluttered room to think in," explains director Martin Scorsese (LEFT). "But in New York, you can't live with that rigor in every room." Raised in Little Italy, he bought a circa 1860 town house on the Upper East Side.

OPPOSITE: Original movie posters adorn nearly every wall of the four-story residence. N. Brodsky's 1937 graphic image for *La Grande Illusion* hangs in the living room. Scorsese, the director of such films as *Taxi Driver* (1976), *Raging Bull* (1980), and *The Aviator* (2004) has been buying posters since 1968.

LEFT: The director views his collection of 16-millimeter films on the projector in the living room. The poster for Renoir's *Le Carrosse d'Or* is from 1953. On the mantel are nineteenth-century Japanese stirrups from actor Ken Takakura.

ABOVE: A Stratocaster played by Robbie Robertson in *The Last Waltz*, Scorsese's 1978 documentary about The Band, is among the collected mementos of his movie career.

The research done by Scorsese's staff for *The Age of Innocence* (1993) gave the director "a greater feeling for Victorian pieces and antiques," notes interior designer Karen Houghton. ABOVE: She divided the second-floor living room into two spaces. Above the circa 1850 English desk are nineteenth-century Japanese wood-block prints from Akira Kurosawa. RIGHT: Bound shooting scripts line the shelves. Scorsese asked for "lots of book space," Houghton notes.

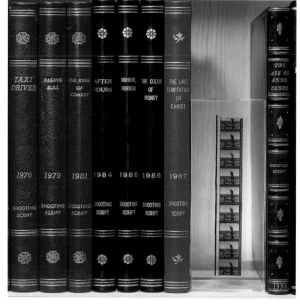

apartments, and I still love the views, but they're not personal enough. I've tried lofts too, and there are beautiful spaces with beautiful light, but the industrial, downtown neighborhoods reminded me too much of the streets where I grew up. When I was living in a loft and editing my films in the same space, I didn't have enough distance from my work. It's not just that you can't close a door: when you're editing a film it seems to permeate your living arrangements. And in the bleaker moments—the moments of despair—it felt as if I'd never left where I came from."

Most modern artists are susceptible to such bleakness, but it's naive to expect that their décor will look like their imagery. Joseph Beuys probably didn't have a blood-stained hyena carcass under his coffee table, and the only artifacts in Martin Scorsese's house that recall

The fantasy of
Cocteau's *La Belle et la Bête*
is portrayed in Jean-Denis
Malclé's 1946 poster.

mean streets are a bottle of grappa and a piece of turquoise pottery from Positano on the sideboard in his dining room. His rooms are warm, decorous, elegant in a manly fashion, and unpretentious. How unpretentious? There's a plaid doggy bed in a corner of his kitchen and a box of tissues on the phone table next to the Eames chair. It looks as if he actually pays his bills at the Victorian desk in his library. He eats alone at a farmhouse table on a well-washed cotton placemat watching the Discovery channel. His dishes are the kind a man buys for himself when his wives have kept the wedding presents.

"Marty has an austere, almost monastic sensibility," says his designer, Karen Houghton. "All his possessions have a personal meaning for him or a reference to one of his movies. He's not a materialist, and since I'm not one either, I think that's one reason we get along." Houghton

met Scorsese through mutual friends in the film world, and she designed his previous apartment—a seventy-fifth-floor space that had a spectacular view and a minimum of furniture. "It was a sleek, cool place," she reflects. "He was up with the hawks, and he could see up the Hudson River. I think Marty needed a warmer life, and here he has one. The house is grounded and complete—it's a welcoming home."

Scorsese says he worked with Houghton the way he would with a production designer. "She came to the set and showed me photographs and swatches, and I made decisions." Houghton describes her client as "very direct and accessible. He has high expectations but he gives you a lot of freedom. He also gave me an excellent definition of what he wanted."

The décor of each floor in the town house has a different mood, adapted to its function. The first-floor

dining room opens to the garden, and Scorsese wanted it to have "a provincial country feeling." The fourth-floor study is the director's lair: he works and reads there, listens to music, screens films, and watches a television that he often keeps tuned to the classic movie channels. "I don't really like television," he admits. The violence? He smiles. "No, that doesn't bother me. It's the commercials, the situation comedies, and the rock videos that are absolutely terrifying."

Houghton's greatest challenge was the open living space on the second floor. The old dumbwaiter shaft, now an elevator, bisects it and couldn't be repositioned, so she created two separate reception areas—"pockets of intimacy," as Scorsese puts it—making the most of the natural light with pale wood floors, ecru walls, and recessed lighting. In the rear is a parlor of subdued Napoleonic elegance that can seat ten or twelve for a screening. In the front is a sophisticated library where the designer has mixed an upholstered sofa with an antique Lavar Kermin rug, a Victorian desk, a wall of bookshelves, and side chairs with an Empire line. "I love the way Marty looks when he sits there," she says. But Houghton was also prepared to integrate the Eames chairs from his last apartment. "He's the right type of person for an Eames chair, and that's not true of everyone. Some men should have their Eames chairs taken away from them."

Filmmaking is a cross between military and court life: it all takes place in public. That's probably why Scorsese is so protective of his privacy. "Between films," he says, "there are days at a time when I don't do anything except hole up and read. My daughters visit, and occasionally there's a guest for dinner—but that's all. And when the work comes in, the time has to be cut out ruthlessly for it."

But what strikes a visitor to Scorsese's town house is less his solitude than his attachments—the power of the presences around him. Director Akira Kurosawa gave him the Japanese prints over the desk and the two ceremonial dolls—an emperor and empress—in the library. A vitrine is filled with talismans and career mementos. Ken Takakura bestowed the samurai stirrups on the mantel in the living room. The guitar hanging like a piece of sculpture on the wall is an original Stratocaster—"a pure one"—that Robbie Robertson played in *The Last Waltz*, Scorsese's 1978 film about The Band. As for the remarkable collection of movie posters hanging in every room and hall, it's only when you've seen *The Age of Innocence* (1993) that you recognize the tone of reverence, authority, and tribal pride that Scorsese adopts when he talks about them. He's an old New Yorker showing you his family portraits.

OPPOSITE: In the dining room is Bernard Lancy's poster for *Les Enfants du Paradis*. "I would never just buy a beautiful poster if I didn't know the film," Scorsese says. "It has to be an extraordinary film, with a special meaning for me." The 1870 dining table is French.

ABOVE: The garden is off the dining room. "I'm not much of a gardener," says Scorsese. "In the tenements I came from we didn't have much room, although those big basil plants did pretty well on the fire escapes."

Frank Sinatra

Inside the Legendary Performer's Palm Springs Compound

TEXT BY DAVID McCLINTICK
PHOTOGRAPHY BY MARY E. NICHOLS
PORTRAITS BY JOHN BRYSON

Palm Springs was one of the most enduring passions of Frank Sinatra's passionate life. Except for his music and his family, Sinatra loved the desert community at the foot of the San Jacinto Mountains longer than he loved anything or anyone else. Although he maintained residences in Los Angeles and New York, they were way stations. Palm Springs was his center, his haven, his home.

Sinatra began frequenting Palm Springs just after World War II, at about the time he won a special Academy Award for a short film on intolerance called *The House I Live In* (1945). He was introduced to the desert by composer Jimmy Van Heusen ("Here's That Rainy Day," "But Beautiful"). Legend has it that Van Heusen, a pilot, had stopped for fuel in Palm Springs and later, over dinner in Los Angeles, told Sinatra of the beauty of the desert. Sinatra insisted that Van Heusen fly him there that very evening.

Other stars were discovering the desert. Sinatra went to parties and dined and danced with Lana Turner and Ava Gardner. He built a house in Palm Springs in 1947 when the town was still small. "We . . . needed our jeep to manage the dirt roads, sand dunes, and tumbleweeds," his older daughter, Nancy, writes in her 1985 book *Frank Sinatra, My Father*. The house was on Alejo Road in the

"Orange is the happiest color," Frank Sinatra said of his favorite hue, which showed up in his clothes and his houses. OPPOSITE: Sinatra bought a modest house at the Tamarisk Country Club in Rancho Mirage in the mid-1950s and lived there until May 1995.

After Sinatra married Barbara Marx in 1976, the couple brought in designer Bea Korshak and architect Ted Grenzbach to renovate the interiors. "Ted made the main house look more solid, less flimsy," said Korshak. LEFT: Sinatra's own paintings hang in the living room.

Canadian businessman Jim Pattison purchased the compound from Sinatra in 1995. ABOVE: Two Sinatra paintings from 1987 hang in the living room.

LEFT: The Sinatras renamed the rooms after his songs. The floor of the painting studio ("Just in Time") still has traces of paint.

fashionable north section, with tall picture windows facing a pool shaped like a grand piano.

In the mid-'50s, with the growing town enveloping his privacy, Sinatra moved. He purchased a small house on a plot of land several miles south and east, on Wonder Palms Road, along the 17th fairway of the new Tamarisk Country Club. It was there that he would establish the home of a lifetime. The small, one-story house had a rough stone entrance and vertical sand-colored clapboard siding. There were two bedrooms, a living room, a tiny kitchen and dining area, and an oval swimming pool open to the golf course. "Sometimes golfers actually walked in," Nancy Sinatra writes. "One clown drove a golf cart right into the pool."

Since there was no immediate fire protection so far out in the country, two huge red fire extinguishers on wheels stood guard over the property. Electrical generators were installed as protection against the frequent power failures. The '50s and early '60s were among the most productive periods of Frank Sinatra's professional life. After winning an Academy Award for *From Here to Eternity* (1953), he made timeless recordings and movies—the albums *Only the Lonely* and *Songs for Swingin' Lovers*, for example, and the films *The Man with the Golden Arm* (1955) and *The Manchurian Candidate* (1962). Between engagements Sinatra gradually expanded his property in the desert to two and a half acres. Having secured privacy with a fence between his

ABOVE: Sinatra's simple bedroom ("I Sing the Songs"), with a double bed, contains many of his possessions: a statue of Saint Francis, a train set, embroidered pillows. Korshak changed some colors to peach, "but I couldn't quite get the orange out of him," she said.

house and the golf course, he added a pair of two-bedroom cottages, one off either end of the pool. Each bedroom had its own separate his-and-her baths. The her baths were equipped with Helene Curtis professional salon hair dryers. Sinatra also expanded the main house, adding a dining room for twenty-four and a restaurant-size kitchen with a commercial range, a walk-in refrigerator and freezer, and a wine closet.

Outside, the desert dweller had a choice: he could keep the natural environment at bay with lush lawns lavishly watered, or he could accommodate his home to its habitat, accepting the sand as lawn, the boulders and cactuses as shrubbery. Sinatra chose the latter, enhancing his terrain with specimen cactuses, saguaro, ocotillo, cholla, and prickly pear, as well as grapefruit, lemon, and lime trees.

John F. Kennedy spent two days at Sinatra's place in 1960, sleeping in a guest room of the main house. Sinatra had a plaque installed to honor the event. When Kennedy became president, it was expected that he would again visit Sinatra, who continued to add to his property: a tennis court, a helicopter pad, a projection room between the main house and the golf course, an office displaying his Oscars, Emmys, Grammys, and gold records, an additional cottage with a bedroom and painting studio, and a four-bedroom bungalow on the west end of the property with a living room, a kitchen, and its own swimming pool. The bungalow, built for his children, was called the Christmas Tree House because of a big pine tree in front.

Kennedy never returned to the Sinatra estate. When the president next visited Palm Springs, he stayed at Bing Crosby's house instead. The Secret Service deemed it more secure. Sinatra was hurt, but by then, over the course of a decade, he had created an utterly singular home for himself and his family—a cluster of plain, anti-style structures, at one with the desert on the outside, and on the inside luxurious, loaded with creature comforts, but homey, not opulent. This was where Frank Sinatra came to rest, read, paint, listen to music, watch movies, play with his model trains (they had their own house—a simulated depot), and entertain his friends and family.

"It was the place of the happiest times we ever had with him," says his younger daughter, Tina. "That was his home, and you could feel it. It was full of great times. I met the *world* in that house."

The nine guest bedrooms at the Sinatra compound were occupied much of the time. The visitors were Hollywood royalty and American and European high society: Noël Coward. Elizabeth Taylor. Richard Burton. Bennett Cerf. Rosalind Russell. Yul Brynner. Dr. Michael DeBakey. The Ronald Reagans. The Milton Berles.

OPPOSITE ABOVE: In the projection room ("Send in the Clowns") are portraits of friends Nat King Cole, Debbie Reynolds, and Ronald Reagan. OPPOSITE BELOW: A hall in the "New York, New York" cottage was lined with Sinatra's art collection; later it held posters from his films.

ABOVE: "The projection room had gold draperies and a busy carpet," said Korshak. "We redid it very simply, with a lot of off-white textured fabrics." The singer's first painting is displayed over the mantel (a print of it is in his bedroom).

"You had no idea who would show up," recalls Daniel Melnick, the film producer and former president of MGM and Columbia Pictures. "It could be the president of the United States. It could be Vito Musso, the great sax player from the Stan Kenton band. Vito, Frank, and Jilly Rizzo would cook their favorite pastas."

"It's well known that [Frank's] the single greatest host since Perle Mesta," writer-director Garson Kanin told Nancy Sinatra. "He got up at five o'clock every morning and he worked like a goddamned Yankee innkeeper

ees, knowing of his love for trains, gave him an actual caboose, in which he installed a sauna, a massage table, a barber chair, an exercise bench, and a huge Toledo scale. His guests used the caboose frequently—hairdressers and masseurs were brought in when needed.

First-run movies were shown in the projection room on studio-quality equipment by studio projectionists imported from Los Angeles. When the New York writer and columnist Sidney Zion was in residence, he asked to see *The Manchurian Candidate*. Sinatra sat with him while he watched it. When the radio personality and novelist Jonathan Schwartz came for an evening, the group watched Marlon Brando and Jack Nicholson in *The Missouri Breaks*, with Frank Sinatra supplying anticipatory plot narration to his guests, a habit he had picked up from the old Hollywood moguls.

In 1976, three years after a career hiatus and three years before *Trilogy*, the biggest recording project of his life, Frank Sinatra married Barbara Marx, another long-time lover of the desert and resident of Palm Springs. The arrival of the new Mrs. Sinatra reminded Mr. Sinatra that his home had been aggressively lived in for more than two decades. It needed work. Barbara Sinatra retained her longtime friend, Beverly Hills interior designer Bernice Korshak, known as Bea, who in turn summoned architect Ted Grenzbach. They opened and lightened the central spaces of the main house and added a master suite for Barbara with travertine floors, a Jacuzzi tub, an exercise room, and lots of mirrors. They also renovated the projection room, which, as the center of constant entertaining, showed the most wear.

As they planned the changes, Bea Korshak and Barbara Sinatra found themselves, with Frank Sinatra's blessing, waging a gentle war on orange. As his favorite color, orange pervaded the property. There was orange carpeting and orange tile, an orange refrigerator and orange draperies, orange towels and an orange sofa. Korshak erased a good deal of orange from the living room and bar of the main house, and from the projection room, substituting subtle desert colors and whites. She blended new window treatments and wallcoverings, as well as furniture.

Outside, Korshak replaced more than a dozen clashing patterns of pool and lawn furniture with a single design of white with brown leather strapping. The buildings on the estate had been named for such frequent guests as Bennett Cerf and Yul Brynner. After the renovation, Frank and Barbara Sinatra renamed each building, and each room within, for Frank's recordings. The main house became "The House I Live In"; the projection room, "Send in the Clowns."

all day to see that everybody had the right number of toothpicks."

And the right amount of music. The entire property was wired for sound. A Bösendorfer concert grand piano, a gift from Jimmy Van Heusen, later given to Nancy, adorned the living room of the main house. A Yamaha upright stood ready in the projection room.

Sinatra's restaurant-strength kitchen was open around the clock, the staff ready to prepare almost any type of food or drink a guest might desire. Not every demand could be filled instantly, however. Late one night Dan Melnick and Tina Sinatra raided the freezer looking for ice cream and found only two or three flavors of Baskin-Robbins. "I made a joke, the word got back to Frank, and the next weekend he had it stocked with all 31 flavors," Melnick says.

Laundry was done on the premises and returned wrapped in soft paper. In 1971 several of Frank's employ-

LEFT: A gift from some of Sinatra's employees in 1971, the caboose (named "Chicago") became the compound's main hangout. BELOW: Inside the caboose was a full-service salon, complete with a barber's chair, a professional hair dryer, a massage table, a scale, and a sauna.

LEFT: Inside "All Aboard," Sinatra's train room, was a replica of his hometown of Hoboken, New Jersey. "Frank had always collected trains," said Korshak. "He would climb up there and move things around. It's noisier than a real station when everything is running."

BELOW: Sinatra sits beside the pool with actor Yul Brynner, a frequent houseguest and a close friend. The compound eventually grew to include eighteen bedrooms and twenty-three baths. "It was almost a hotel at times," recalled Korshak. "Frank liked having people around him."

A part of the property that changed relatively little was Frank Sinatra's bedroom ("I Sing the Songs"). Though there was new furniture and a new fireplace, the room's essence would remain. There was a plain double bed (not king size) with a headboard covered in orange-and-white fabric. A small statue of Saint Francis stood in a corner. Above the bed was a print of Sinatra's first painting, an orange-and-brown abstract (the original hangs in the projection room). Copper sculptures of train engines rimmed the fireplace, and a Denver Express model train stretched along the mantel. Books filled shelves.

From his room, Sinatra could look out to the pool, monitoring the comings and goings. Or, with the flick of a switch, he could close the shades, plunging the space into pitch blackness for sleeping, essential for a man who worked and played—and then slept—very late.

"He loved that room—it was a little cave," Tina Sinatra says.

On the door to the brown-and-orange dressing area was a small plaque that read: "I believe in the sun even when it's not shining. I believe in love even when not feeling it. I believe in God even when he is silent." The dressing area was small and simple, with a massage table and a steam shower but no bathtub. A mosaic snowman made by Tina Sinatra when she was eight hung on one wall. A panel of clocks gave the time in Los Angeles, New York, London, Hong Kong, and Tokyo. There were two sad-faced clowns, painted by Sinatra, self-portraits. The suite reflected modesty, a lack of ostentation in Frank Sinatra's most private space, so different from his image.

Sinatra sang in public for what would prove to be the last time on Saturday, February 25, 1995—six songs at an annual Palm Springs golf tournament that he and Barbara sponsored for the benefit of the Barbara Sinatra Children's Center. He sang well, considering that he was a seventy-nine-year-old man in failing health. Shortly thereafter, the Sinatras put their estate on the market and prepared to take up full-time residence in their houses in Malibu and Beverly Hills.

The Palm Springs compound was sold to a Canadian businessman, Jim Pattison. The Sinatras' scheduled departure date approached, but Frank Sinatra did not want to leave. Barbara inquired about renting the place for an additional month. Pattison declined but allowed them to stay as guests. Weeks passed. A Pattison representative moved onto the property. Finally, in late May, Sinatra arose one day, breakfasted, showered and shaved, donned a suit and tie, and got into a town car. His staff of twenty-six, informed that he was leaving for good, lined up along both sides of the driveway as a driver eased the car out of the compound and down the street that had long since been renamed Frank Sinatra Drive. A few minutes later a Pattison employee found half a dozen of the female staff sitting and kneeling on the floor of Sinatra's bedroom quietly crying.

Giving up his home devastated Sinatra. He never got over it, and he died in Los Angeles three years later—on May 14, 1998—without returning to the compound. He did come back to the desert, however. His remains are interred alongside his parents' near his former estate.

ABOVE: Sinatra with his dog, Ringo, one of seven dogs and four cats in residence that he rescued from a shelter. The two-and-a-half-acre property was filled with boulders and had citrus trees, ocotillo and saguaro cactuses, and other plants indigenous to the desert.

Steven Spielberg
The Director's Guesthouse in East Hampton

TEXT BY SUZANNE STEPHENS
PHOTOGRAPHY BY NORMAN MCGRATH

Steven Spielberg has found that having both fame and good architecture exacts a common price: it is harder and harder to be left alone. It's not just all those Oscars. It's also the guesthouse that he and his wife, actress Kate Capshaw, built in East Hampton. "We would love to use the guesthouse for ourselves, but it has attracted so many guests that we're the strangers on the property," quips Spielberg about the addition to the residence that he and Capshaw share with their seven children.

The guesthouse, designed by architect Charles Gwathmey of Gwathmey Siegel & Associates, is the third component of a secluded Long Island compound that began to take shape in the mid-1980s. At that time Gwathmey moved an eighteenth-century Pennsylvania Dutch barn from New Jersey to a site overlooking a large pond, renovating it for Spielberg's main house. He also

Architect Charles Gwathmey designed a cedar-shingled guesthouse for the East Hampton residence of film director Steven Spielberg (above) and his family.
OPPOSITE: Seen from the arbor, the guesthouse's gabled skylight caps the gallery, the spine of the structure. "Each building expresses a unique program and scale," says Gwathmey of the compound.

LEFT: Gwathmey had previously converted an eighteenth-century Pennsylvania Dutch barn ("the referential volume") into the main house.

designed a gatehouse in a simple farmhouse vernacular and placed it on the other side of the pear orchard facing the barn.

The decision to build a guesthouse posed the problem of how it should be designed to fit in with the ensemble of shingled farm-style buildings. "We didn't want it to look like a miniature barn," says Gwathmey. Nor did he and Spielberg think the guesthouse should dominate the field of vision in this serenely pastoral setting bordered by a lush growth of vines, privet, and climbing roses. "We thought it should be a one-story building," the architect says. "It's not visible from the road, but it establishes a low horizontal edge, to the site." "However," noted Naomi Leff, the late New York City interior designer whom Gwathmey had previously worked with and suggested for this project, "Steven didn't want the guesthouse to be a lesser version of the barn; he wanted it to be equal in design quality."

Since the main house, a.k.a. Quelle Barn, looms up on the smooth, grassy lawn as a single volumetric entity, stalwart and indomitable, Gwathmey designed the guesthouse as a linear assemblage of smaller-scale geometric forms. From the cleanly curved corner of the exercise room to the crisply rectilinear projections of the pavilionlike bedrooms to the semicircular bowed window of the living room, each space in the guesthouse is differentiated architecturally. "The exterior allows you to read the change of functions inside with great clarity," Gwathmey emphasizes.

Having form follow function properly satisfies the architect's modernist impulse, while the articulation of the mass gives the structure an intimate scale more characteristic of traditional architecture. Yet Gwathmey makes it clear that he is not replicating history. "The design of the guesthouse does not try to refer to the barn and its particular aesthetic," he says. "I wanted to explore an interpretation of a traditional context while maintaining the integrity of a modern work."

The guesthouse's varied roofline and, in turn, the changing ceiling contours within, are as important as the enclosing walls in precluding the possibility that the one-story house would look like another "ranchburger." As with the modulated walls, the shapes of the roofs help indicate the different functions: single-pitched roofs over the bedrooms, a pyramidal one topping the living room, and an elongated glass gable for the gallery skylight.

The pyramidal roof hovers above the living room, effecting a sheltering hut. Its thickly textured, sloping timber-frame ceiling gives the room a sense of both spaciousness and security. The architecturally discerning eye might also appreciate the manner in which the heavy square base of the roof's pyramid appears to float over the curved window wall.

BELOW: The guesthouse was designed as a villagelike assemblage of geometric forms.

OPPOSITE: All of the bedrooms open onto the skylit gallery—Spielberg's favorite area of the house—which displays the framed artwork of young visitors. "It's an enormously fun space," said interior designer Naomi Leff.

"I used muted colors to tie in all the different styles of art and furniture," Leff said. "I was also playing off the teal-blue trim of the architecture." LEFT: The living room palette softens the effect of the pyramidal timber-frame ceiling. "The best thing about Naomi's interior design was the selection of fabrics and their hues, even more than their textures," says Spielberg.

LEFT: A circa 1862 rooftop finial is installed as a piece of sculpture in the dining area, furnished with Gustav Stickley table and chairs. The brick floor, French doors, and plants contribute to the indoor-outdoor character.

ABOVE: Gwathmey planned the kitchen as an "open, participatory space." A circa 1875 folk-art horse-head mold complements the mahogany cabinetry and the stone countertops. The lamps carry over from the gallery.

Dramatic spatial punch also occurs in the skylit gallery connecting the public areas—living room and dining area on one end and gym on the other—with the bedrooms. As Spielberg observes, "The width of the gallery and the amount of light transmitted through the skylight make it my favorite part of the house. And, unexpectedly, it's cool in the midday heat of July." Gwathmey and project architect Jose Coriano saw the gallery as important in unifying the organization of the rooms. "It's like a village, where each programmatic element is articulated, and the spine, acting as a mews, holds the buildings together," Gwathmey explains.

Opening off the gallery are the children's bedrooms and the two master bedrooms. Since each master bedroom has its own fireplace, window seat, and outdoor terrace, along with its own bath, the accommodations resemble bungalows at a resort. On the other side of the gallery, Gwathmey designed the children's bedrooms as enclaves, with four bunk beds abutting snugly at a

corner. "They're meant to be compact, cabinlike spaces, where there is a sense of sharing and of community," he says.

The architecture of each of Spielberg's residences, which include his Mediterranean-style Pacific Palisades house and guesthouse, as well as the East Hampton farmhouse complex, borrows greatly from the vernacular of the region. Yet the interiors are all dominated by Arts and Crafts furnishings, supplemented by American folk art and the occasional Vienna Secession and Art Deco piece. Interestingly, maintaining the thematic mix in the different architectural idioms proves to be successful, as does combining different periods of furniture that share a simplicity and straightforwardness of form. "Folk art and country furniture work well with Arts and Crafts," Leff said, citing the nineteenth-century rooftop finial installed as a sculpture in the dining area, the plank-top sofa table in the living room and the Stickley-style beds in the master bedrooms.

"Since Arts and Crafts furniture can be strong and powerful," Leff said, "and the house is low and horizontal, I tried to keep the mood somewhat soft and romantic." This she did with a palette of pale green, peach, and teal blue. "Naomi had one of the best color senses of anyone I've met," says Spielberg. "She'd have made a fine cinematographer."

Leff, who was assisted by Virginia Cornell, was Gwathmey's choice for the interiors because "we could have a dialogue," he says. "It's not about my taste versus your taste. But it is about how to reconcile various points of view. The only thing I asked of Naomi was to underdo it a bit—to edit the pieces and support the architecture."

The architectural expression appears to have hit the right chord with the owner. As Spielberg puts it, "Charlie has dared himself to be different with both the barn and the guesthouse. I think he has surprised a lot of peo-

ple in the architectural community by showing he is a designer of many personalities."

For their parts, the architect and the interior designer recognize the value of having a client as creative as Spielberg. "Working with Steven is great because he is visual, yet he also believes in collaboration," says Gwathmey. Said Leff, "People like Steven understand the discipline it takes to keep from losing the idea along the way, so that you end up with something that has integrity and a certain amount of purity." In other words, good architecture.

ABOVE: "It was conceived as a miniature house," says Gwathmey of one of the master bedrooms, which opens to its own terrace. The blanket chest is antique.

"The children's bedrooms are about intimacy and a sense of sharing," Gwathmey says. OPPOSITE: A Matthew Imperiale rug is the focal point in a children's bedroom, where the bunk beds meet in ship's-cabin style.

"The guesthouse completes the framing of the site by the architecture," Gwathmey comments. OPPOSITE: The dining area of the guesthouse looks southward across the terrace and lawn to the Spielbergs' main house, which the family has dubbed Quelle Barn. ABOVE: "It's kind of an inversion," notes Gwathmey of the bowed projection of the living room onto the terrace. "You feel like you could be outside of the building." Random-width oak planks, tongue-and-groove cedar siding, and the fireplace brick maintain a continuity with the exterior. A pair of Josef Hoffmann chairs near the fireplace and, at left, a Dirk van Erp lamp behind the sofa are part of the Spielbergs' collection of Vienna Secession and Arts and Crafts furnishings. RIGHT: Gwathmey designed the exercise room, placed away from the main living areas at the west end of the gallery, as "a loft, accommodating a variety of equipment," he says. The audio-visual wall is built-in.

James Stewart

The Star of *It's a Wonderful Life* and *The Philadelphia Story* in Beverly Hills

TEXT BY A. SCOTT BERG
PHOTOGRAPHY BY MARY E. NICHOLS

He was born on May 20, 1908, at home, in a small town. There—in Indiana, Pennsylvania, where the Alleghenies begin their gentle ascent—he also worked in his father's hardware store, joined the Boy Scouts, made model air-planes and played the accordion. And though he pro-ceeded to become one of the most successful actors of his time—and arguably the most beloved movie star of all time—James Stewart never left that small town behind him. He brought its basic values of serving God, country, community, and family through hard work to many of his movie roles, infusing his modest, life-size film characters with elements of his own character.

BELOW: James Stewart and his wife, Gloria, look over papers in the study in 1951. The year before had been one of the actor's busiest: four films, including *Harvey* and *Winchester '73*, were released. OPPOSITE: The house on Roxbury Drive in Beverly Hills, where the actor lived for nearly fifty years, had changed little since he bought it in 1949.

LEFT: A profile sketch of Pie, the horse Stewart rode in *Broken Arrow* (1950) and *How the West Was Won* (1962), hangs in the entrance hall. Although Stewart seemed completely natural on screen, Alfred Hitchcock, who directed him in *Rear Window* (1954) and *Vertigo* (1958), described him as "a painstaking craftsman."

OPPOSITE: The cowboy in the living room was for his induction into the Hollywood Westerners Hall of Fame.

Stewart attended his father's alma mater, in a small town in New Jersey. While majoring in architecture at Princeton University, he found himself drawn to the campus's most colorful extracurricular activity—the Princeton Triangle Club, which produced an original musical comedy every year.

Upon graduation in 1932 Stewart received an invitation to Falmouth, a small seaside town in Massachusetts, from another Triangle alumnus, Joshua Logan, who belonged to a summer stock company called the University Players. Stewart joined a remarkable array of young talent there, including an actor from Nebraska, Henry Fonda. The season had barely ended when a producer invited Stewart to reprise one of his roles at the Biltmore Theatre on Broadway. One theater job led to another, and in 1934 he screen-tested for MGM. The following summer he went to Hollywood, entering the ranks of the first generation of talking-picture actors.

Hollywood was a small company town unto itself, and MGM was the most productive—and glamorous—factory in the industry. In less than three years Stewart's boy-next-door looks and slight stammer and drawl catapulted him to leading-man status. Like most young contract players, Stewart made some of the most important leaps in his career on loan-out to other studios. One such deal was to Columbia Pictures in 1939, playing the eponymous hero in *Mr. Smith Goes to Washington*.

The role seemed tailored to Stewart's background, that of a small-town, idealistic Everyman, a former scout who could utter a lot of nationalistic sentiment with complete conviction. While he failed to win the Oscar for which he was nominated, the role permanently enshrined him as a monument to democracy.

The following year he played a cynical reporter who, in the course of covering a society wedding, falls in love with the bride himself. Stewart received his second Academy Award nomination for *The Philadelphia Story* and was as surprised as most when he won. Many considered it a consolation prize for *Mr. Smith*, but its star, Katharine Hepburn, felt otherwise. The performance, she said, showed that "nobody could speak his heart on film better than Jimmy."

The next five years should have been the most productive in Stewart's film career, but World War II intervened. After logging extra hours in his own plane so that he might enter the war as a military pilot, he spent four years training pilots and flying bombing raids over Germany. He returned a highly decorated colonel and later became a brigadier general in the air force reserve.

Back in Hollywood, Stewart opted out of the MGM contract that awaited him. Frank Capra promptly approached him again, this time with a story about a self-sacrificing Everyman who is shown the way out of his desperation one Christmas by an angel in quest of his

RIGHT: Photographs of family
and friends cover the piano
in the living room. "Dad
learned piano from his
mother when he was a
boy," says his daughter
Kelly Stewart. "After dinner
parties he would play and
sing 'Ruth,' 'I've Got a
Crush on You,' and 'Ragtime
Cowboy Joe.'"

"I've never been a Holly-
wood glamour boy,"
claimed Stewart (below),
who starred in nearly eighty
films. Signed by MGM in
1935, he was first cast in
The Murder Man, with
Spencer Tracy. "I told him
to forget the camera was
there," said Tracy. "That
was all he needed."

wings. The role of George Bailey of Bedford Falls—its
streets not much different from those of Indiana, Pennsylvania—earned Stewart his third Oscar nomination.
He did not win, and *It's a Wonderful Life* (1946) was not
big box office. But decades later it proved to be a holiday
evergreen, practically making Jimmy Stewart as integral
to the yuletide as Santa Claus.

As though life were imitating art, Stewart almost
instantly duplicated the loving family with which he had
just performed. In 1949, at the age of forty-one, he wed
Gloria Hatrick McLean, a beautiful divorcée with a sharp
wit and a raucous laugh that preceded her into a room.
She brought two young sons, Ronald and Michael, to the
marriage and less than two years later gave birth to twin
girls, Judy and Kelly. By then Jimmy and Gloria had
found a way to live a small-town life despite his big-
screen career.

Behind silver birches on the 900 block of Roxbury
Drive in Beverly Hills sat their unpretentious Tudor-
influenced, two-story family house. The cozy foyer led to
two formal rooms: On the right was a large living room,
with a few French pictures and a grand piano, at which
Jimmy occasionally performed his deadpan rendition of
"Ragtime Cowboy Joe." To the left was the dining room,
with an oak table and a French provincial bookcase serving as breakfront. Except on holidays and a few festive
occasions, the Stewarts rarely used either room.

Instead, the family gathered each evening in the library
beyond the living room. Almost every surface in this informal room was covered with some article of memorabilia.
Wildlife, a family passion, provided the prevailing theme
of the objets d'art. And on an easel sat a portrait of Pie,
Stewart's horse in numerous westerns, as rendered by
Henry Fonda. Stewart used to prepare for family vacations
by putting valuables in a vault—not jewelry and silver, but
the family photograph albums from this room.

On the other side of the house, beyond the dining
room and next to the kitchen, sat the breakfast room,
where the Stewarts took all their meals. Jimmy had
held on to its wood picnic-style table from his bachelor
days; and it was only after many years that more
rigid chairs replaced the canvas director's chairs that
once surrounded it. Everybody served himself from a
lazy Susan.

As seemed required of every movie-star house, the
Stewarts had a private screening room. Theirs, however,
was little more than a finished basement rumpus room,
with a 16-millimeter projector at one end, which Jimmy
used to insist on threading himself, often fumbling for
the better part of an hour, whenever he wanted to run a
movie at home.

A yellow carpet led upstairs from the foyer to a long landing that divided the second story into two distinct wings. The children lived on the north side of the house—the boys sharing one twin-bedded room, the girls another. The south side of the house contained the master suite—a large bedroom with a comfortable sitting area. Here one found the house's few concessions to glamour—separate baths and dressing areas. Her dressing room was large enough for a sofa and chairs, but her bath did not even have a full-size tub. His bath was even more basic—a pedestal sink and a small tile shower, with a dressing room not much bigger than a broom closet.

The property's greatest distinction was outside. The day the house next door came up for sale in the '60s, Stewart bought it and promptly razed it, folding in the entire lot, producing a great expanse of lawn with big trees. Gloria created a magnificent flower and vegetable garden, filling the salad bowl every night. After dinner she and Jimmy used to walk their golden retrievers around the block, sometimes going for a "two-blocker." The Stewarts regularly attended the nearby Presbyterian church—where Gloria taught Sunday school—always returning to the same pew.

With his extraordinary range as an actor, Stewart was able to star in films for almost five decades. He proved equally at home in moody westerns, frothy domestic comedies, and four Alfred Hitchcock suspense pieces, including *Rear Window* (1954) and *Vertigo* (1958); he portrayed such all-American heroes as Glenn Miller and Charles Lindbergh. He received his fourth Oscar nomination for playing small-town dipsomaniac Elwood P. Dowd, sorting out reality with a six-foot rabbit in *Harvey* (1950); his fifth for playing small-town attorney Paul Biegler, arguing for a man's life in *Anatomy of a Murder* (1959). He brought a gentle canniness to all the roles, a sly worldliness just when one expected corny provincialism to set in.

The '70s and '80s were filled with television appearances, successful stage revivals of *Harvey*, lifetime achievement awards, charity events, the constant flow of fan mail, even a best-selling book of poems. He was always willing to pose for photographs and to sign autographs—"part of the job," he insisted. Into the '90s Gloria got him out at night as often as possible.

With little warning, Gloria Stewart died of lung cancer in 1994. Jimmy increasingly withdrew, hardly leaving their house, seeing few beside his family. Three years later—on July 2, 1997—he developed a blood clot in his lung.

A genuine icon, the last of the men from Hollywood's Golden Age, that first generation of talking-picture stars, James Stewart died peacefully that morning in the same bed his wife had—at home in a small town.

TOP: A New York Film Critics Award for Stewart's 1959 film *Anatomy of a Murder*, which also earned the actor his fifth Academy Award nomination, is displayed at the bar. Other mementos—including a Bendix Air Race trophy—reflect his lifelong love of flying.

ABOVE: The Stewarts shared an interest in wildlife conservation. The giraffe sculpture is an award for their service to the Natural History Museum of Los Angeles. Photographs depict the Jimmy Stewart Museum in the actor's hometown of Indiana, Pennsylvania.

OPPOSITE: Stewart's Oscars—for Best Actor in *The Philadelphia Story* in 1940 and for Lifetime Achievement in 1984—are displayed in a niche in the library. On the wall is a 1939 New York Film Critics Award for Stewart's classic early role in *Mr. Smith Goes to Washington.*

LEFT: "The library was the most used room in the house," says Kelly Stewart. "Family and friends always gathered there before dinner." On the low table are a Presidential Medal of Freedom, the nation's highest civilian honor, and a book of poems Stewart published in 1989.

LEFT: Henry Fonda, one of Stewart's first roommates after he moved to Hollywood, created the still life on the easel in the master bedroom. Fonda once said of the Stewart residence, "It's as comfortable as Jimmy, with a splash of style thrown in by Gloria."

John Travolta and Kelly Preston

The Actor Parlays His Passion For Airplanes into a Bold Family Home in Florida

TEXT BY NANCY COLLINS

PHOTOGRAPHY BY DURSTON SAYLOR

"It was always John's dream to have planes in his front yard—to practically be able to pull up to the house—so that when you wanted to go to dinner, all you'd have to do was step out the door, get on the plane, and whisk off," Kelly Preston says of her aviation-mad husband. "And we fly in and out a lot. Last year when Johnny was shooting a movie in Tampa, he flew to and from work every day. Each night the kids and I would go out in the golf cart, watch the landing, then bring Johnny to the house while the plane taxied in. It was very exciting."

John Travolta has always been dotty about flying. In fact, when the Hollywood superstar talks about his childhood jaunts, those romantic days when plane etiquette demanded that he "wear a sport coat and tie, my mom and sister white gloves"—his tone grows positively reverential. "The TWA Terminal at Kennedy was only two years old—and I, ten—when I first flew into it on a 707 from Chicago," he recalls. "And then at fifteen, when I got my first look at Dulles International, well, it just took me."

And how. Three decades and millions of logged miles later, John Travolta not only pilots planes but is the proud owner of two—both of which he likes keeping near enough to touch, much less fly. "When I was a kid, I imagined that by the turn of the century everyone would have his own plane in the backyard," he says. "That didn't happen, so we're hoping to provide inspiration."

Not to mention awe. After all, fellow travelers, it's not every day that you sit in somebody's living room and gaze through 25-foot windows into the face, make that nose, of a 135-foot 707 jet from Qantas, nor for that matter, a comparatively modest Gulfstream II. But that is exactly the case in the spectacular 8,900-square-foot concrete-and-glass air palace of John Travolta and Kelly Preston—a futuristic cross between the hippest '50s pad and the hippest airport on the planet.

"Building a home might be the most difficult challenge anyone encounters, and I'm not making light of how hard this was," admits Travolta. "It took me eight years to get it going." But then, the actor had requirements few homeowners run up against—like a 7,500-foot runway. Travolta eventually found it on four hundred acres—eight of which he snapped up—in Ocala, Florida, originally used for the airlifting of wild animals kept on the property. "I moved here, primarily, to have the bigger, stronger runway," he says of his spread, "then built a taxiway that would endure the weight of the 707."

That curious design chore solved, the couple turned their attention to an unusual host of others—starting with the view. "Looking from the inside—or out—we

BELOW: "I can't call it modern—it's really a mid-century-style home," actor John Travolta says of the Florida house he shares with his wife, actress Kelly Preston. "Thank God Kelly was such a good traveler and liked to fly as much as I did," remarks the actor. OPPOSITE: A games table in the great room.

ABOVE: John Adams, of Land Design Group, used tropical vegetation by the pool. RIGHT: Curved window walls define the great room, which looks onto the tarmac. Above the mantelpiece is a 1967 work by Alexander Calder.

wanted to have a view of both aircraft," explains Preston, "to see them from the bedroom, the great room, the dining room." As a result, both carriers, noses safely tucked under individual plane ports, as it were, sit a mere hundred feet from the house, allowing its owner to taxi almost up to his front door. Once he disembarks, two outdoor walkways lead directly into the heart of the house.

A project this original called for an open-minded architect—especially since the couple knew exactly what they wanted. "Having sat with this for thirty-five years, I had a very specific vision, modern but elegant— a house that could have been created during the era when the great hotels and terminals were built, 1952 to '62. The biggest job for Dana Smith was listening to our ideas, essentially mocking up our imaginations," a process jump-started by the detailed sketches and plan drawn up by the couple themselves.

The inspiration for the six-bedroom main house, as well as a 6,500-foot garage complete with eight efficiency apartments, came from three distinct architectural styles: the clean lines and dark woods of Frank Lloyd Wright; the aeronautical elegance of Eero Saarinen, designer of the Dulles and TWA terminals; and Morris Lapidus, architect of Miami's Fontainebleau Hilton Resort, whose loftily curved lobby windows served as prototype for the towering blue-tinted windows (eighteen and fifteen feet in bedroom and dining room) that swathe the Travoltas' main edifice.

ABOVE: His vintage Thunderbird is in the front drive of the residence, which was designed by architect Dana Smith. RIGHT: A Gulfstream II jet is parked in one of two plane pavilions. Although the property came equipped with a 7,500-foot runway, Travolta extended the taxiway to reach the house.

"John had a vision of how he wanted everything to be," says designer Sherri James, of Michael James Design Team in Southern California. "We just implemented his ideas." OPPOSITE: Travolta designed the floor motif in the entrance hall.

Despite glass grand enough to ogle a jet (whose thirty-foot tail makes it as tall as the house itself), Kelly Preston knew that the surest way to people's hearts remains the stomach, not the cockpit. "We started with the kitchen," says Travolta, a man as passionate about food as flying, "because, as Kelly pointed out, everybody ends up near the food." Anticipating this inevitability, the Travoltas built two kitchens, one for serious cooking, another for lighter fare, surrounding them with three individual dining areas "that spit out from the kitchen," explains Travolta, "like those in great hotels."

Floating artfully throughout the great room are crisp, low-slung sofas and contemporary hollow-backed Italian chairs in soothing hues of aqua and chartreuse. "The sea greens against the blue-tinted windows," says Preston, "all blend into each other, seeming to go on endlessly into the sky."

LEFT: The bath has a poster from *Pulp Fiction*. Construction of the house lasted two years, but "the plan took, on and off, about six years," Travolta says. "We moved into the guest quarters for a while to oversee it." OPPOSITE: Family photographs, books, and airplane models are displayed on shelves in the main hall.

"This is an overbuilt home," Travolta says. "The walls are thicker than they need to be, and there's more metal in it than there needs to be." LEFT: The master bedroom "is serene," James observes.

THE AIRLINES OF THE UNITED STATES
* * *
ALASKA AIRLINES, INC.
ALL AMERICAN AVIATION, INC.
AMERICAN AIRLINES, INC.
AMERICAN EXPORT AIRLINES, INC.
BRANIFF AIRWAYS, INC.
CHICAGO AND SOUTHERN AIR LINES, INC.
COLONIAL AIRLINES, INC.
CONTINENTAL AIR LINES, INC.
DELTA AIR LINES
EASTERN AIR LINES, INC.
INLAND AIR LINES, INC.
MID-CONTINENT AIRLINES, INC.
NATIONAL AIRLINES, INC.
NORTHEAST AIRLINES, INC.
NORTHWEST AIRLINES, INC.
PAN AMERICAN AIRWAYS, INC.
PAN AMERICAN-GRACE AIRWAYS, INC.
PENNSYLVANIA-CENTRAL AIRLINES CORP.
TRANSCONTINENTAL & WESTERN AIR, INC.
UNITED AIR LINES, INC.
WESTERN AIR LINES, INC.

"Michael Eisner was our first dinner guest," says Travolta. "He looked at our planes and said, 'My God, I get it. Within an hour we can be on our way to Paris.'" LEFT: Sandra Hilliard copied the mural in the dining room from a 1937 advertisement in *Fortune*.

BELOW: Travolta's office features his Qantas 747 pilot certificate, his American Airlines Boeing 707 pilot certificate, an award for excellence in aviation from the American Institute of Aeronautics and Astronautics, and a photograph of the actor in his ultralight over Florida.

For the Art Deco dining room, the couple eschewed the '50s for the '30s—beautifully evidenced by the dazzling fifteen-foot-by-seventeen-foot mural featuring a family dressed to the nines awaiting their flight—an advertisement that Travolta, a collector of old magazines, culled from a 1937 *Fortune*. "I'd been waiting years to do something with this picture until it hit me: historically, murals were used in dining rooms, and this would be perfect."

Preston's main concern, meanwhile, was comfort, "since this was a family where kids play on the sofa, watch TV, hang out with us." And Jett and Ella, says their mother, "love it because it's a fun house. We've got a big pool, a slide, a golf course . . . we're a family who likes to play a lot." Off or on board. While some might pitch a tent in the backyard, the Travolta kids have the option of a sleepover in a 707.

"The kids are great fliers," says Travolta, who adds that Jett has been known to stay on board after a flight, watching videos while the crew cleans up. Ella, meanwhile, recently experienced the thrill of her first commercial flight. "She was like, 'Ma, Ma? Who are all these people on the plane?'" her mother laughs. Adds Travolta, "She was so excited to tell me, 'Daddy, there's things called tickets!'" Indeed, if Ella has her way, she may someday be sitting at the controls next to her father. "Barbra Streisand asked Ella what she wanted to

ABOVE: An exterior view takes in the length of the house. Travolta restored the exterior of the Boeing 707 (opposite, far right), which was built for Qantas in 1964. "You can be the ultimate eccentric, like I am, and bring in a 707," he says. "But you can also bring in any corporate jet or airliner."

be when she grows up," says Preston, "and she said: 'A pilot. Like my daddy.'"

The Travoltas admit that they made some "bold choices—the same as with a movie," says the actor. "Making *Face/Off*, every day I said to Joan Allen and Nic Cage, 'This is either going to be the worst—or most original—thing anyone's ever seen.' And it turned out great. It's the same with homes. You don't know but have to take the risk to break new ground."

Indeed. And would they have done anything differently? "If I'd made my gates wider, I wouldn't have to maneuver so much," Travolta laments, a comment that makes his wife chuckle. "He's talking about electric gates that most people drive a car through, opening up to bring in a 707."

That said, surely the couple must be gobsmacked by what they have pulled off? Do they ever look around . . . the two planes parked in their yard and just . . . giggle?

"Oh, yeah," they laugh in unison. "Every single day."

RIGHT: "The pool cabana is a grownup playroom," says James. "John wanted to use it for dancing, which is why it has a big open space and stone flooring." A 1989 painting shows his Learjet.

Jack L. Warner

The Beverly Hills Estate of the Archetypal Hollywood Mogul

TEXT BY CHARLES LOCKWOOD
PHOTOGRAPHY BY JEFFREY HAYDEN

Of all the estates created by Hollywood "greats" in Beverly Hills during the 1920s and '30s, just one—the Jack L. Warner residence—remains complete with its original mansion and extensive grounds.

Only a handful of Beverly Hills houses have ever rivaled the Warner estate. With its 13,600-square-foot Georgian-style mansion, expansive terraces and gardens, two guesthouses, nursery and three hothouses, tennis court, swimming pool, nine-hole golf course, and motor court complete with its own service garage and gas pumps, the nine-acre property was—and still is—the archetypal studio mogul's estate.

Few residences, moreover, compared with the Warner estate as a social milieu in the '30s and '40s. "I remember one New Year's Eve party in 1939 or 1940," Olivia de Havilland recalled. "All the men were glorious in white tie. Errol Flynn was behind the bar, Howard Hughes was my date, and Jimmy Stewart was seated on a stool. Just the four of us having our first drink of the evening. All those beautiful women dressed in wonderful elegance. Dolores del Rio in a white satin gown that contrasted her dark hair and dark eyes. Ann Warner, herself a striking presence. Those beautiful women, looking marvelous in this wonderful setting."

Unlike most of his famous neighbors, Warner did not build his estate in one grand gesture. Instead, he created his home step-by-step over an entire decade according to the changes in his business affairs and personal life.

This estate, like so many other studio moguls' residences, was the symbol of Warner's hard-won success. The sons of a Polish immigrant shopkeeper, Jack, Harry, Albert, and Sam Warner entered the movie business when they purchased a nickelodeon in Newcastle, Pennsylvania, in 1904. Jack Warner entertained the audiences during intermissions. During the next two decades the Warners expanded into film distribution with varying degrees of success, and in 1923 they formed Warner Bros.

In the early '20s Warner Bros. had been a distinctly second-rank studio, whose best-known star was Rin Tin Tin. At times, the studio was so hard-pressed that Warner left his office by the back door in order to avoid

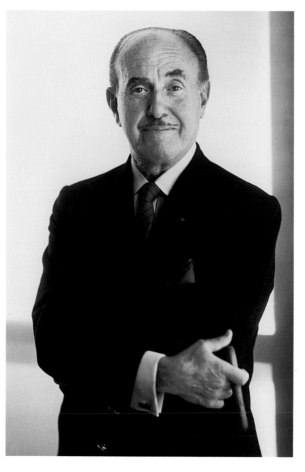

"I am what I am, and I will probably never change," wrote Jack L. Warner (left), head of the Warner Bros. Studio for over forty years and the 1958 recipient of the Irving G. Thalberg Memorial Award.
OPPOSITE: On his nine-acre estate, which he built from 1926 to 1937, was a Neoclassical mansion designed by architect Roland E. Coate with interiors by William Haines and grounds by Florence Yoch.

creditors. But by 1926 he felt comfortable enough to purchase three acres of former farmland in the gentle foothills a half mile north of the Beverly Hills Hotel and to start construction of a house. Two years later, Warner and his family moved into a new fifteen-room Spanish colonial–style mansion.

Within several years, however, the residence seemed inadequate to Warner. The studio's financial condition had improved considerably after its highly profitable introduction of the talkies with *The Jazz Singer* (1927). Warner Bros. subsequently enjoyed a string of financial and critical successes with gangster films like *Little Caesar* (1930) and *Public Enemy* (1931), the Busby Berkeley musicals, and social-conscience movies like *I Am a Fugitive from a Chain Gang* (1932). Warner had become so rich that he bought an adjacent parcel of land that had

been subdivided into building lots, and installed a pitch-and-putt golf course with two ponds. He then acquired—and demolished—three nearby mansions and added those lots to his estate. (The three houses, it is estimated, would today have cost ten million dollars.)

Warner completed the grounds of his spectacular estate in 1937, a year after his second marriage, to Ann Page, an occasional screen actress.

The existing Spanish-style mansion, which had been the height of architectural chic in the mid-'20s, looked outdated by the mid-'30s, and it reminded the brash studio head of his failed first marriage. Warner consequently enlisted architect Roland E. Coate, who

enlarged and rebuilt the mansion in the Georgian style with an impressive Greek Revival portico. Coate was well known in the conservative San Marino and Pasadena social circles during the '20s, but after designing producer David O. Selznick's nearby residence, he had begun in the '30s to work more and more in flamboyant Beverly Hills.

In keeping with the Warner mansion's elegantly restrained façade, matinee-idol-turned-designer-to-the-stars William Haines decorated the rooms in a Georgian style, frequently adding his own whimsical touches. Haines counted some of the '30s and '40s Hollywood legends among his clients, including Joan Crawford and

ABOVE: Adjoining the sunroom and off the entrance hall was the main living room, which contained a fraction of the Warners' antiques, such as George III mahogany armchairs, a George III–style library table and cut-glass chandelier, and an early George III lady's writing desk, right. Under the arched doorways are two sets of eighteenth-century Chinese painted wallpaper panels.

Douglas Fairbanks, Jr., Carole Lombard, Norma Shearer, and director George Cukor. He also helped popularize the Neoclassical style in Los Angeles residences during the '30s.

At the Warner mansion, the front door opened into a two-story entrance hall, notable for its extraordinary parquetry floors with patterns executed in a variety of woods and a sweeping cantilevered staircase that led to the upstairs bedrooms.

On the first floor, the living room boasted eighteenth-century English paneling, corner niches for the display of Wedgwood china and other objects, and a George III-style cut-glass chandelier. The room, like most of the others, displayed a number of fine antiques, including a George III–style mahogany library table and a George III writing desk.

With its parquetry floor, wall niches, Adamesque serving table, and early-nineteenth-century French wallpaper with picturesque scenes of India, the dining room

typified William Haines's pleasing style. The multi-pedestal dining table usually sat sixteen at dinner parties, but it could be expanded to accommodate several dozen guests. The Warners owned a set of no less than forty-eight Regency-style dining chairs.

The library could seat several dozen as comfortably as a private screening room. The sunroom had handsome paneling in the Gothic style that was so popular in late-nineteenth-century England, and its furniture was a mixture of fine Chippendale pieces and large, comfortable sofas and chairs. A portrait of Ann Warner painted by Salvador Dalí and celebrated with a party for about three hundred people was set into the paneling over the fireplace mantel.

An invitation from the Warner estate replaced one from Pickfair as the most sought after in the '30s and '40s movie community, but the reason was not Warner's warmth or goodwill. Although Warner was a brilliant businessman, he was widely feared for his ruthless practices in a rough-and-tumble Hollywood, and he was

BELOW: In the dining room, decorated with early-nineteenth-century wallpaper panels, a table is surrounded by fourteen of the Warners' forty-eight Regency-style armchairs, George III mahogany urns and pedestals, right, and a Carrara-marble-and-lapis-lazuli mantel-piece, left.

LEFT: The screening room had several concealed devices, including projectors hidden behind a panel that was opened by moving the Buddha's head.

BELOW: The screen was raised with the help of a water pump, and the front sofa was rotated for viewing.

OPPOSITE: Louis XV–style painted panels decorated the library, which contained hand-bound leather volumes of every movie script Warner Bros. produced.

OPPOSITE: Warner made many editing decisions for his studio's movies from this George II walnut wing chair in his home screening room.

RIGHT: Next to the screening room was the bar, which was ornamented by two monumental 1760 Mexican candlesticks and a circa 1820 Mexican chandelier. Behind the bar are Tang Dynasty pottery and figures; in the center is a statue of Guanyin, of whom Ann Warner was a devotee. Her interest in Buddhism was reflected in Guanyin figures throughout the house.

often mocked behind his back for his bad jokes. His invitations were rarely refused, however, because he headed one of Hollywood's most powerful studios, which had been awarded Best Picture Oscars for *The Life of Emile Zola* (1937) and *Casablanca* (1943), and whose stars included Errol Flynn, Humphrey Bogart, Lauren Bacall, Al Jolson, James Cagney, and Bette Davis, who was famous for fighting with her headstrong boss.

For most people, a Sunday at the Warner estate meant a visit to the grounds but not to the house—except for the Hollywood elite or young actresses who visited the studio boss during his wife's frequent absences. Still, what splendid grounds landscape architect Florence Yoch created for the Warners, far grander than those of the residences of her other Hollywood clients, such as David O. Selznick and George Cukor.

The estate's gates opened onto a winding driveway, lined by sycamores, that proceeded up the hill and ended at the brick-paved motor court. On one side stood the mansion's porticoed entrance, its whiteness and Neoclassicism a handsome contrast to the heavily landscaped grounds. On the other side of the motor court, Yoch installed an elliptical fountain, followed by a series of landscaped terraces decorated with urns and statues, another fountain with statues of Cupid riding a sea horse, and finally a seventeenth-century-Italian-style colonnade in front of an ivy-covered wall.

In other parts of the estate, Yoch designed terraces with wide views of the city, garden-lined stairways from the house to the tennis court and swimming pool, water cascades, and a fern grotto. The Warner estate, quite fittingly, was landscape architecture at its theatrical best.

The property was more than a verdant Shangri-la; it was a veritable country club. The swimming pool area had two enormous terraces, one with several lounge chairs, the other with an outdoor kitchen, barbecue, and soda fountain. Warner enjoyed his lighted tennis court year round, and doubles matches were a feature of the Sunday parties. Golf was another favorite pastime. As it turned out, the Warners' next-door neighbor, silent-screen comedian Harold Lloyd, also had a nine-hole pitch-and-putt course on his estate. Warner occasionally erected a temporary walkway over the wall between the two estates so that he and his guests could play all eighteen holes.

Although the Warners hosted fewer and fewer afternoon parties in the '50s, they still welcomed old friends and such younger stars and entertainers as Elizabeth Taylor, Tony Curtis, Janet Leigh, Frank Sinatra, Judy Garland, Paul Newman, Doris Day and Merv Griffin.

In the '50s and early '60s Warner continued to rule the studio with an iron hand, and Warner Bros., which won the Best Picture Academy Award for *My Fair Lady* (1964), expanded profitably into television production.

Florence Yoch, the set designer and landscape designer who was responsible for the grounds at David O. Selznick's and George Cukor's estates, created a dramatic setting for the Warner residence. ABOVE: The mansion had multiple fountains and a series of landscaped terraces. "One of the greatest points of interest in building gardens in California is the variety of materials available to harmonize with the many styles of architecture," Yoch wrote.

OPPOSITE: In addition to a nine-hole pitch-and-putt golf course, the estate had a large swimming pool, around which the frequent Sunday afternoon guests would lounge.

In 1967, at age seventy-five, Warner sold his interest in the studio, and over the next several years he gradually retired from the motion picture industry.

After Jack Warner's death in 1978 at age eighty-six, Ann stayed at the estate, amid significant changes in the neighborhood. Many of the area's '20s and '30s mansions were modernized or torn down. Others, like Harold Lloyd's Greenacres, remained standing but lost most of their grounds. Only the Warner estate escaped these fates.

When Ann Warner died in 1990, record mogul David Geffen purchased the property and the mansion's furnishings for an estimated $47.5 million. Ann and Jack Warner's home of five decades—the last intact estate from Hollywood's Golden Age in Beverly Hills—broke national records for the sale of a single-family residence.

John Wayne

Best Actor for *True Grit* in Newport Beach

TEXT BY SAM BURCHELL
PHOTOGRAPHY BY FRITZ TAGGART

The house in Newport Beach, California—though it occupied a splendid setting at the water's edge facing Balboa Island—was simple and unpretentious. There was nothing to suggest that it was the private world of a superstar and an American legend.

Nevertheless, John Wayne lived there for sixteen years, after moving south from a five-acre ranch in Encino. He had long been familiar with Newport Beach, and he remembered the days when it was no more than a village. "I came down here to live fourteen years ago," he said in 1977. "I sure as hell couldn't afford it now."

Wayne's reference to real estate prices in Orange County was appealingly direct. There was, in fact, nothing indirect about John Wayne at all—or about his house. Pretensions were better left outside, somewhere along the Pacific Coast Highway.

Nothing, however, is that simple, and Wayne's personality was no exception. He was a man far more complex, far more sophisticated, and far more sensitive than his archetypal screen image might suggest. For example, his house meant a great deal to him, and it was hardly a place to throw down the saddlebags and kick a bedroll into the corner.

Wayne's study presented the clearest image of the man himself. It was warm, generous, and comfortable, most definitely a man's room. The paneling, the fireplace, and the small collection of guns strengthened the feeling, and there were many fine examples of Western American art as well as Native American artifacts. A collection of kachina dolls, for example, was begun in the days when Wayne used to ride into Monument Valley in Arizona to make films. Everywhere in the study were the memorabilia of his remarkable career.

The walls around the desk contained innumerable photographs and plaques marking the notable events of his life. Rising above a shelf on which stood the Oscar he received for his performance in *True Grit* was a wall Wayne called the "50 Years of Hard Work Wall." It was also a record of memories and friendships: pictures of his children; a faded photograph of himself with John Ford,

Henry Fonda, and Ward Bond, proudly displaying a sailfish caught near Cabo San Lucas in the early 1930s.

The mementos, the awards, the trophies—all attested to the variety of places Wayne visited, whether on location or traveling for pleasure. And for more than thirty years, in the course of those travels, he collected furniture and art and objects of all kinds.

There were porcelain jardinieres from Honolulu and figures from Bali, acquired just after World War II, when the area was relatively unknown. There were antiques he found in Colorado Springs, furniture from Madrid, figurines from Kyoto, and a good deal of Alaskan art.

When Wayne was on location, nothing gave him more pleasure than spending his free time browsing through whatever antiques shops were available. His curiosity led him to many an unlikely place. On the

ABOVE: John Wayne, whose acting credo was "I don't act, I react," lived in Newport Beach, California, amid antiques and mementos he'd collected from all over the world.

RIGHT: A Baccarat chandelier is reflected in the mirrored dining room wall above a Nepalese deity.

The design of Wayne's house embodied his direct and personal style. RIGHT: A gilt-bronze Buddha stands before a stone fireplace wall amid contemporary paintings in the living room. On the Chinese table, a broncobuster and pony express rider by Harry Jackson adds western elements.

terrace at Newport Beach there was a porcelain table with a pedestal base that he found in one of the poorest sections of Puerto Vallarta. While making a film in Fort Benning, Georgia, he came across a favorite Empire table. His interest in collecting was a compelling one, and it was his habit to take treasured prints or small antiques with him on location.

"You often have to stay for a couple of months in some horrible motel room," he said. "Well, I like to put a few familiar things on the wall. I try to dress the place up a little, make it seem more like home."

He was, of course, happiest when back at his house in Newport Beach. "Look," he said, "I find things that

ABOVE: A hallway is lined with photographs, including one at lower left with Fay Wray as mascot for a charity football team of Hollywood's leading men in the 1930s.

appeal to me and I try to blend them in here. I don't give a damn whether anyone else likes them or not. But I think I've done a pretty fair job."

There was no mock modesty in these words, but there was more than a hint of understatement. The words say a good deal about John Wayne. They evoke a particularly human image—the image of a man of taste and sensitivity, deeply interested in his family and in his home. Perhaps in the last analysis this is a larger and more solid image of John Wayne than the familiar one seen on all the film screens of the world.

ABOVE: The master bed-room, with its views of Newport Bay.

LEFT: Wayne liked to call his bayside view "not a scene, but a 'moving picture.'"

ABOVE: The atrium off of the living room featured two ceramic storks from Vietnam.

RIGHT: In the wood-paneled den, a collection of kachina dolls lines the fireplace wall. The group of running horses on the low table is a bronze by Cynthia Rigden.

Orson Welles

The Maverick *Citizen Kane* Creator in New York

BY SIMON CALLOW

Orson Welles's career is often deceptive. In 1938, for instance, when he bought his spanking-new duplex on 57th Street, it seemed as if he were on top of the world. The Mercury Theatre, which he had created with John Houseman only a year before, had immediately written itself into theatrical history with its dazzling first season. Starting with their famously audacious production of *Julius Caesar* in jackboots, they had gone on with scarcely less aplomb to the little-known *Shoemaker's Holiday* by Shakespeare contemporary Thomas Dekker (a riotous tour de force in Welles's hands) and Shaw's difficult *Heartbreak House*. Welles himself was a radio star of the first magnitude, both as the Shadow in the popular series of that name—supposedly anonymous, but anonymity and Welles were opposed concepts—and as the helmsman, director, leading actor, and prime mover of *Mercury Theatre on the Air*. Having fielded a number of stunning adaptations of classic melodramas in state-of-the-art productions, the series had brought the nation to a momentary halt with the broadcast of H. G. Wells's *War of the Worlds*, which was aired on Halloween eve 1938. A part of the huge audience for the Charlie McCarthy show, unimpressed by the talents of that evening's vocalist, had accidentally tuned in halfway through the Mercury broadcast to what they took to be a sober newscast describing the invasion of New Jersey by martians.

Welles's face would soon be on the front page of nearly every newspaper in the world. Even the irrepressible twenty-three-year-old Boy Wonder of the American Theater—as he had long ago been dubbed after his sensational "voodoo" *Macbeth*, all of two action-packed years before—was a little taken aback by what he'd unleashed. His already considerable reputation swelled to monumental proportions—as much for his showmanship as for artistic achievement. He seemed to be able to get away with anything.

In reality, Welles was in serious trouble. *War of the Worlds* had come in the middle of a nightmarish technical rehearsal period for the Mercury production of *Danton's Death*, the opening play of its second season. No sooner had Welles—more or less—extricated himself from the mayhem (protests, lawsuits, outraged editorials)

caused by the martian broadcast than he was opening a production of an enormously challenging play complicated by a set that hadn't been thought through and a lighting plot that had never had a chance of working. The show was a mild flop, though not a critical disaster. New York's theatrical community was therefore amazed when Welles and Houseman precipitately wound up the Mercury. What had seemed to be the brightest hope there

OPPOSITE: Though considered one of the industry's most influential filmmakers, Orson Welles won his only Academy Award for the screenplay of his first film, *Citizen Kane* (1941), sharing the honor with Herman J. Mankiewicz. He went on to make *The Magnificent Ambersons* (1942), *Othello* (1952), and *Chimes at Midnight* (1965). In 1938 and 1939 Welles lived in a modern duplex on East 57th Street in New York City with his wife, actress Virginia Nicolson, and their daughter, Christopher. RIGHT: The entrance hall. BELOW: Welles painted the living room murals and designed the furniture himself.

had ever been for that great dream, an American national theater, was summarily dashed.

For Welles and Houseman there was a new radio program, *The Campbell Playhouse*, sponsored by the well-known soup manufacturer (Houseman observed that they presumably figured that "if we could sell the end of the world, we could certainly sell tomato soup, too") in addition to the prospect of offers from Hollywood. Studio bosses had already flirted with Welles—as actor, as literary adviser, as possible director. But he was holding out for a much bigger prize. He wanted the lot. Actor-writer-director Orson Welles was his radio sobriquet; he could see no reason why it shouldn't be repeated in film. He was in no rush, however. He and Houseman had a final debt to discharge to the Mercury and to the

theater a massively ambitious enterprise that would cover the whole of Shakespeare's history cycle condensed into two evenings under the title *Five Kings*.

It was at about this point in his life that Welles bought a duplex on East 57th Street. He was clearly in an expansive mood; the duplex was by no means cheap, and it represented a substantial step upmarket. His first New York apartment in the mid-1930s had been over a grocery store on 14th Street; spreading the newspapers about this impossibly tiny space, he had managed to set fire to both them and it. With his first proper money from radio, he, his young wife, actress Virginia Nicolson, and their somewhat capriciously named daughter, Christopher, had moved into an inexpensive rented house in Sneden's Landing on the other side of the Hudson from Tarrytown.

Of Welles, John Barrymore once quipped, "He's an exhibitionist, a publicity seeker, a headline hunter, a cheap sensationalist . . . Why, he's another John Barrymore!" ABOVE AND OPPOSITE: "The dining area was set on a balcony overlooking the living room," Virginia Nicolson Pringle recalled in 1996.

Following his success with the Mercury Theatre in New York, Welles went to Hollywood at twenty-four and signed a contract to write, act in, direct, and produce a film a year. "I didn't want money," he said. "I wanted authority." RIGHT: Welles plays with Christopher, his eldest daughter, in New York.

The couple had previously rented a house in Sneden's Landing, from which Welles would travel by boat and chauffeur-driven Rolls-Royce into the city to work. Among the Mercury Theatre's radio broadcasts was the infamous dramatization of H. G. Wells's *War of the Worlds*. LEFT: Welles's office.

This had been the cause of much journalistic comment, not so much on the house itself as on the lifestyle that seemed to go with it. To come into town Welles would take a motorboat across the water; once off the ferry, he would be greeted by a chauffeur-driven Rolls (ancient and broken-down, he defensively insisted). Lunch would be at his club, '21.' There he would be shaved and manicured, then he would go on into the mad whirl of his life—the meetings, the suppers, the rehearsals in the theater, the recordings in the radio studio, the all-night drinking. Perhaps it no longer made sense to him to waste all that time on the boat and in the Rolls (although he used to claim that he could get from his doorstep to Times Square in half an hour); perhaps he simply wanted to be nearer to the center of things.

The duplex (the fashionable dwelling of the moment) was just on the edge of the Upper East Side, next to the Swedish restaurant where he and his wife frequently dined, not far from the exclusive elegancies of Sutton Place; the world-renowned soprano Lily Pons lived in the duplex next door. Cool, open, ruthlessly rectilinear, the apartment was absolutely up-to-the-minute. As such, it seems an odd home for the romantic throwback that was Welles. The fact is, according to Virginia Nicolson, he was rarely there and had left the furnishing of the apartment largely to her. Its function was emblematic: an appropriate setting for the brilliant young couple. There

was a piano and an organ—both hauled up from the first floor through the huge dining area window—but Welles played neither; they were for his wife. He had no interest in cooking, so the splendidly equipped kitchen remained unvisited: "What," he asked Nicolson plaintively, "does water look like when it's boiled?" His principal contribution to the apartment had been to decorate the walls. An inspired illustrator—his *Everybody's Shakespeare* edition of three of Shakespeare's plays with stage directions and his own drawings, which was first published when he was nineteen, was now a standard school textbook—he painted Mediterranean vistas, framed by pillars and arbors. He also designed the unusual furniture, huge chairs and sofas, made for him by a theater carpenter, to complement the stained-glass windows and the balcony dining room, which could only be reached by means of a staircase.

The apartment seems in an odd way—though on a much smaller scale and in an entirely different style—to prefigure Charles Foster Kane's Xanadu: there is the same aspiration to domestic gigantism, with the intention presumably of lending weight and substance, but dwarfing even the largest human figure.

He was not to stay in the apartment for very long, anyway. *Five Kings* turned out to be a monumental folly, dogged by technical and artistic problems. The tour broke down in Philadelphia after a catastrophic run.

Welles then embarked on a suicidal tour of the variety circuit in a twenty-minute abridgment of that hoary old mock-melodrama *The Green Goddess*. He was lucky to play to more than a half a dozen people a night.

At what was unquestionably the nadir of Welles's career to date, something that even he would never have dreamed of, turned up: the most famous contract in movie history, the contract that eventually resulted in the 1941 film *Citizen Kane*. His lawyers and managers had been quietly negotiating with George J. Schaefer, the new head of RKO; finally Schaefer gave in and signed the

deal that gave Welles final cut on his first film, which he would write, produce, and direct. He swiftly moved to Hollywood and just as swiftly fell in love with Dolores del Rio. So the last use of the 57th Street apartment was for him to break the news to his wife that he was moving to California permanently and that he wanted a divorce. Xanadu was sold, the murals painted over, and the huge chairs shipped out. It was the end of the first phase of Welles's life.

Welles's film style was both strikingly visual and extremely intuitive. "I think I share with Hitchcock the ability to say what lens goes in the camera and where it stands without consulting a finder or looking in the camera," he said. "I just walk over and say, 'There it is.'"
ABOVE: The bedroom.

Contributors

A. Scott Berg is the author of *Kate Remembered*, a biography of Katharine Hepburn, and *Goldwyn: A Biography*, and is the winner of the American Book Award and the Pulitzer Prize.

John Bryson has photographed numerous celebrities for such magazines as *LIFE*, *Newsweek*, and *People*.

Sam Burchell was a former senior editor for *Architectural Digest*.

Simon Callow is an actor (appearing in such films as *Four Weddings and a Funeral* and the HBO miniseries *Angels in America*), director, screenwriter, and author, having written biographies of Orson Welles and Charles Laughton.

Charles Champlin is a former arts editor and columnist for the *Los Angeles Times*. His books include *George Lucas: The Creative Impulse* and *Hollywood's Revolutionary Decade*.

Gerald Clarke, an *Architectural Digest* contributing writer, is the author of *Capote*, a biography of Truman Capote, and *Get Happy*, a biography of Judy Garland.

Nancy Collins, an *Architectural Digest* contributing writer, is a former ABC News correspondent and the author of *Hard to Get: Fast Talk and Rude Questions Along the Interview Trail*. She lives in New York.

Loomis Dean is a photographer who created memorable images as a staff photographer for *LIFE* magazine.

Michael Frank, an *Architectural Digest* contributing writer, lives in New York City.

Joseph Giovannini, a practicing architect, is an *Architectural Digest* contributing writer and an architecture critic for *New York* magazine.

Allan Grant has photographed numerous celebrities and historical figures and is a former staff photographer for *LIFE* magazine.

Lawrence Grobel is the author of *The Art of the Interview: Lessons from a Master of the Craft*, *The Hustons*, *Conversations with Capote*, and *Conversations with Brando*.

Gray Horan, Greta Garbo's only grandniece, is a freelance writer.

Dena Kaye is a journalist and the president of the Danny Kaye and Sylvia Fine Kaye Foundation.

Charles Lockwood is the author of books about American architecture and cities, including *Dream Palaces: Hollywood at Home* and *The Estates of Beverly Hills*.

Russell MacMasters is a designer and photographer.

David O. Marlow is an *Architectural Digest* contributing photographer. His images appear in *Art of Grace and Passion: Antique American Indian Art*, and he is currently working on a book about Aspen houses.

David McClintick, the author of *Indecent Exposure: A True Story of Hollywood and Wall Street*, is writing a biography of Frank Sinatra.

Cynthia McFadden is a correspondent and anchor for ABC News.

Norman McGrath's photographs have illustrated *Manhattan Skyscrapers* and *New York's Pennsylvania Stations*, among other books. He is also the author of *Photographing Buildings Inside and Out*.

Jim McHugh is an *Architectural Digest* contributing photographer and is known for his work in the art community. He has published *California Painters: New Work* and *The Art of Light + Space*.

John Meroney, a writer and producer in Los Angeles, is at work on a book about Ronald Reagan's Hollywood career. He has written for *The New Republic*, *Forbes FYI*, the *Sunday Telegraph*, *The Washington Post*, *The Wall Street Journal*, the *Los Angeles Times*, and the *Houston Chronicle*.

Mary E. Nichols is an *Architectural Digest* contributing photographer. Her photographs have appeared in *Blair House: The President's Guesthouse*.

Robert Reck is an *Architectural Digest* contributing photographer whose most recent book is *Facing Southwest: The Life and Houses of John Gaw Meem*.

Durston Saylor is an *Architectural Digest* contributing photographer. His images have appeared in numerous books, including *Michael Graves: Buildings and Projects 1990–1994* and *Skidmore, Owings & Merrill LLP: Architecture & Urbanism 1995–2000*.

Donald Spoto has written biographies of Marilyn Monroe, Marlene Dietrich, Laurence Olivier, Alfred Hitchcock, Ingrid Bergman, and Tennessee Williams.

David Stenn is the author of *Clara Bow: Runnin' Wild* and *Bombshell: The Life and Death of Jean Harlow*.

Suzanne Stephens is the author of *Imagining Ground Zero: Official and Unofficial Proposals for the World Trade Center Site*.

Tim Street-Porter is an *Architectural Digest* contributing photographer and the author of *Tropical Houses*, *Freestyle*, *Casa Mexicana*, and *The Los Angeles House*.

Fritz Taggart has photographed the work of numerous interior designers and was a frequent contributor to *Architectural Digest* and the *Los Angeles Times*.

Judith Thurman, an *Architectural Digest* contributing writer, is the author of the biographies *Isak Dinesen: The Life of a Storyteller*, which won a National Book Award, and *Secrets of the Flesh: A Life of Colette*. She writes regularly for *The New Yorker*.

Michael Webb, an *Architectural Digest* contributing writer, is the author of eighteen books, including *Modernism Reborn: Midcentury American Houses*, *Richard Sapper*, and *Beach Houses*.

Theo Westenberger, an *Architectural Digest* contributing photographer, is based in New York.

Photo Credits

Candice Bergen (appeared in October 1999 issue): page 10 by Jim McHugh; pages 11–17 by Robert Reck

Humphrey Bogart and Lauren Bacall (April 1990 issue): pages 18–19, 20 (below) by MPTV.net; pages 20 (above), 21 by Sid Avery/MPTV.net

Cher (August 2002 issue): page 23 by Ken Nahoum; pages 22, 24–29 by Mary E. Nichols

George Cukor (Jan./Feb. 1978 issue; reprinted April 1990): pages 30–37 by Russell MacMasters Photography

Cecil B. DeMille (March 1987 issue; reprinted April 1990): page 39 by Marc Wanamaker/Bison Archives; pages 38, 40–45 by Mary E. Nichols

Clark Gable and Carole Lombard (April 1990 issue): pages 46–47 (above) courtesy Academy of Motion Picture Arts and Sciences; pages 48–49 Bettman/CORBIS

Greta Garbo (April 1992 issue): pages 50, 54 (above), 57 (above) by David Hays/© Gray Reisfeld; pages 51–53, 55, 57 (below) by Fritz von der Schulenburg/© Gray Reisfeld; page 54 (below) by Clarence Sinclair Bull/Courtesy Gray Reisfeld; page 56 by Billy Cunningham/© Gray Reisfeld

Judy Garland (April 1992 issue): pages 58 (above), 61 (above), 62 courtesy Sid Luft; pages 58 (below), 59, 60 (below), 61 (below), 63–65 by The John Fricke Collection; page 60 (above) courtesy Itasca County Historical Society, Garland Gallery, Karjala Research Center, Grand Rapids, Minnesota

Cary Grant and Randolph Scott (April 1996 issue): pages 66–71 by Wisconsin Center for Film and Theater Research

Jean Harlow (April 1994 issue): page 72 by Grimes/Courtesy Academy of Motion Picture Arts and Sciences; pages 73–75, 77 (above) © Turner Entertainment Co., A Warner Bros. Entertainment Company. All Rights Reserved/Courtesy Academy of Motion Picture Arts and Sciences; page 76 by MGM/The Kobal Collection/Bull, Clarence Sinclair; page 77 (below) courtesy David Stenn

Katharine Hepburn (April 1990 issue; reprinted in July 2004): page 79 by Ernest A. Bachrach/© Turner Entertainment Co., A Warner Bros. Entertainment Company. All Rights Reserved; pages 78, 80–83 from *The Private World of Katharine Hepburn* by John Bryson. © 1990 by John Bryson (text and photographs); ©1990 by Katharine Hepburn (foreword). By permission of Little, Brown and Company, Inc.

Anjelica Huston and Robert Graham (April 1996 issue): page 84 by Robert Graham; pages 85–93 by Tim Street-Porter

John Huston (April 1992 issue): pages 94–99 by Loomis Dean

Danny Kaye (November 2001 issue): pages 101 (below), 102 (below) courtesy The Kaye Family Archives; pages 100–01 (above), 102 (above), 103–07 by Tim Street-Porter

Diane Keaton (April 2005 issue): page 111 by Firooz Zahedi; pages 108–10, 112–15 by Tim Street-Porter

Jayne Mansfield (April 1996 isssue): pages 116–25 by Allan Grant

Marilyn Monroe (April 1994 issue): page 126 by MPTV.net; page 127 by Bob Beerman and Bert Parry/George Zeno Collection; page 128 © 2005 Milton H. Greene Archives, Inc. www.archivesmhg.com; page 129 by Robert W. Kelley/TLP/Getty Images; page 130 by Paul Adrian/ Courtesy Academy of Motion Picture Arts and Sciences; pages 131–32 by The James Haspiel Collection; page 133 by Allan Grant

Dennis Quaid (October 2003 issue): pages 134–43 by David O. Marlow

Ronald Reagan (April 2000 isssue): page 145 (below) courtesy Academy of Motion Picture Arts and Sciences; page 146 (above) from the Personal Collection of Nancy and Ronald Reagan; page 147 (above) courtesy G.E.; pages 144, 145 (above and center), 146 (below), 147 (below) courtesy Ronald Reagan Presidential Library

Martin Scorsese (April 1994 issue): pages 148–55 by Durston Saylor

Frank Sinatra (December 1998 issue): pages 156, 162, 164 (below), 165 by John Bryson; pages 157–61, 163, 164 (above) by Mary E. Nichols

Steven Spielberg (November 1994 issue): page 167 (above) © Jonathan Levine; pages 166, 167 (below), 168–75 by Norman McGrath

James Stewart (April 1998 issue): pages 176, 180 (below) © Turner Entertainment Co., A Warner Bros. Entertainment Company. All Rights Reserved/Courtesy Academy of Motion Picture Arts and Sciences; pages 177–80 (above), 181–83 by Mary E. Nichols

John Travolta and Kelly Preston (April 2004 issue): pages 184, 194 (below) by Theo Westenberger; pages 185–93, 194–95 (above), 195 (below) by Durston Saylor

Jack L. Warner (April 1992 issue): page 196 © Warner Bros. Entertainment Inc. All Rights Reserved/Courtesy USC Cinema-Television Library and Archives of Performing Arts; pages 197–205 by Jeffrey Hayden

John Wayne (October 1977 issue; reprinted in April 1990): pages 206–11 by Fritz Taggart

Orson Welles (April 1996 issue): page 212 Everett Collection; page 215 (above) Culver Pictures, Inc.; pages 213–14, 215 (below), 216–17 The Billy Rose Theatre Collection/The New York Public Library for the Performing Arts/Astor, Lenox and Tilden Foundations

Index